Bob Woodcock

ESSENTIALS

OCR GCSE
Biology A

Ideas about Science

The OCR Twenty First Century Biology specification aims to ensure that you develop an understanding of science itself – of how scientific knowledge is obtained, the kinds of evidence and reasoning behind it, its strengths and limitations, and how far we can rely on it.

These issues are explored through Ideas about Science, which are built into the specification content and summarised over the following pages.

The tables below give an overview of the Ideas about Science that can be assessed in each unit and provide examples of content which support them in this guide.

Unit A161 (Modules B1, B2 and B3)

Ideas about Science	Example of Supporting Content
Cause–effect explanations	Genetics and Lifestyle (page 6)
Developing scientific explanations	Genetic Information (page 4)
The scientific community	Evolution by Natural Selection (page 31)
Risk	Testing Fetuses (page 8)
Making decisions about science and technology	The Implications of Genetic Testing (page 9)

Unit A162 (Modules B4, B5 and B6)

Ideas about Science	Example of Supporting Content
Data: their importance and limitations	Collecting Data about how Light Affects Plants (page 44)
Cause–effect explanations	Limiting Factors for Photosynthesis (page 43)
Developing scientific explanations	Memory (page 64)
Making decisions about science and technology	Stem Cells (page 52)

Unit A163 (Module B7)

Ideas about Science	Example of Supporting Content
Data: their importance and limitations	Monitoring and Assessing Progress (page 70)
Cause–effect explanations	Injuries Caused by Excessive Exercise; Sprains (page 71)
Developing scientific explanations	Learning from Natural Ecosystems (page 77)
The scientific community	Monitoring and Assessing Progress (page 70)
Risk	Medical History Assessment (page 69)
Making decisions about science and technology	Sustainable Development (page 80)

Data: Their Importance and Limitations

Science is built on data. Biologists carry out experiments to collect and interpret data, seeing whether the data agree with their explanations. If the data do agree, then it means the current explanation is more likely to be correct. If not, then the explanation has to be changed.

Experiments aim to find out what the 'true' value of a quantity is. Quantities are affected by errors made when carrying out the experiment and random variation. This means that the measured value may be different to the true value. Biologists try to control all the factors that could cause this uncertainty.

Biologists always take repeat readings to try to make sure that they have accurately estimated the true value of a quantity. The mean is calculated and is the best estimate of what the true value of a quantity is. The more times an experiment is repeated, the greater the chance that a result near to the true value will fall within the mean.

The range, or spread, of data gives an indication of where the true value must lie. Sometimes a measurement will not be in the zone where the majority of readings fall. It may look like the result (called an 'outlier') is wrong – however, it doesn't automatically mean that it is. The outlier has to be checked by repeating the measurement of that quantity. If the result can't be checked, then it should still be used.

Here is an example of an outlier in a set of data:

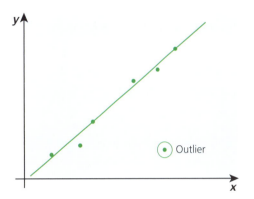

Outlier

HT The spread of the data around the mean (the range) gives an idea of whether it really is different to the mean from another measurement. If the ranges for each mean don't overlap, then it's more likely that the two means are different. However, sometimes the ranges do overlap and there may be no significant difference between them.

The ranges also give an indication of reliability – a wide range makes it more difficult to say with certainty that the true value of a quantity has been measured. A small range suggests that the mean is closer to the true value.

If an outlier is discovered, you need to be able to defend your decision as to whether you keep it or discard it.

Ideas about Science

Cause–Effect Explanations

Science is based on the idea that a factor has an effect on an outcome. Biologists make predictions as to how the input variable will change the outcome variable. To make sure that only the input variable can affect the outcome, biologists try to control all the other variables that could potentially alter it. This is called 'fair-testing'.

You need to be able to explain why it's necessary to control all the factors that might affect the outcome. This means suggesting how they could influence the outcome of the experiment.

A correlation is where there's an apparent link between a factor and an outcome. It may be that as the factor increases, the outcome increases as well. On the other hand, it may be that when the factor increases, the outcome decreases.

For example, in plants, there's a correlation that up to 40°C, the higher the temperature, the greater the rate of photosynthesis.

Just because there's a correlation doesn't necessarily mean that the factor causes the outcome. Further experiments are needed to establish this. It could be that another factor causes the outcome or that both the original factor and outcome are caused by something else.

The following graph suggests a correlation between going to the opera regularly and living longer. It's far more likely that if you have the money to go to the opera, you can afford a better diet and health care. Going to the opera isn't the true cause of the correlation.

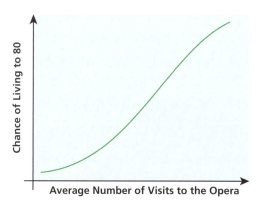

Sometimes the factor may alter the chance of an outcome occurring but doesn't guarantee it will lead to it. The statement 'the more time spent on a sun bed the greater the chance of developing skin cancer' is an example of this type of correlation, as some people will not develop skin cancer even if they do spend a lot of time on a sun bed.

To investigate claims that a factor increases the chance of an outcome, biologists have to study groups of people who either share as many factors as possible or are chosen randomly to try to ensure that all factors will present in people in the test group. The larger the experimental group, the more confident biologists can be about the conclusions made.

HT Even so, a correlation and cause will still not be accepted by biologists unless there's a scientific mechanism that can explain them.

Developing Scientific Explanations

Biologists devise hypotheses (predictions of what will happen in an experiment), along with an explanation (the scientific mechanism behind the hypotheses) and theories (that can be tested).

Explanations involve thinking creatively to work out why data have a particular pattern. Good scientific explanations account for most or all of the data already known. Sometimes they may explain a range of phenomena that weren't previously thought to be linked. Explanations should enable predictions to be made about new situations or examples.

When deciding on which is the better of two explanations, you should be able to give reasons why.

Explanations are tested by comparing predictions based on them with data from observations or experiments. If there's an agreement between the experimental findings, then it increases the chance of the explanation being right. However, it doesn't prove it's correct. Likewise, if the prediction and observation indicate that one or the other is wrong, it decreases the confidence in the explanation on which the prediction is based.

The Scientific Community

Once a biologist has carried out enough experiments to back up his/her claims, they have to be reported. This enables the scientific community to carefully check the claims, something which is required before they're accepted as scientific knowledge.

Biologists attend conferences where they share their findings and sound out new ideas and explanations. This can lead to biologists revisiting their work or developing links with other laboratories to improve it.

The next step is writing a formal scientific paper and submitting it to a journal in the relevant field. The paper is allocated to peer reviewers (experts in their field), who carefully check and evaluate the paper. If the peer reviewers accept the paper, then it's published. Biologists then read the paper and check the work themselves.

New scientific claims that haven't been evaluated by the whole scientific community have less credibility than well-established claims.

It takes time for other biologists to gather enough evidence that a theory is sound. If the results can't be repeated or replicated by themselves or others, then biologists will be sceptical about the new claims.

If the explanations can't be arrived at from the available data, then it's fair and reasonable for different biologists to come up with alternative explanations. These will be based on the background and experience of the biologists. It's through further experimentation that the best explanation will be chosen.

This means that the current explanation has the greatest support. New data aren't enough to topple it. Only when the new data are sufficiently repeated and checked will the original explanation be changed.

HT You need to be able to suggest reasons why an accepted explanation will not be given up immediately when new data, which appear to conflict with it, have been published.

Ideas about Science

Risk

Everything we do (or not do) carries risk. Nothing is completely risk-free. New technologies and processes based on scientific advances often introduce new risks.

Risk is sometimes calculated by measuring the chance of something occurring in a large sample over a given period of time (calculated risk). This enables people to take informed decisions about whether the risk is worth taking. In order to decide, you have to balance the benefit (to individuals or groups) with the consequences of what could happen.

For example, deciding whether or not to have a vaccination involves weighing up the benefit (of being protected against a disease) against the risk (of side effects).

Risk which is associated with something that someone has chosen to do is easier to accept than risk which has been imposed on them.

Individuals might also be more willing to accept risks that have short-term effects rather than long-lasting ones.

HT Perception of risk changes depending on our personal experience (perceived risk). Familiar risks (e.g. smoking) tend to be underestimated, whilst unfamiliar risks (e.g. a new vaccination) and invisible or long-term risks (e.g. radiation) tend to be overestimated.

For example, many people underestimate the risk of getting type 2 diabetes from eating too much unhealthy food.

Governments and public bodies try to assess risk and create policy on what is and what isn't acceptable. This can be controversial, especially when the people who benefit most aren't the ones at risk.

Making Decisions about Science and Technology

Science has helped to create new technologies that have improved the world, benefiting millions of people. However, there can be unintended consequences of new technologies, even many decades after they were first introduced. These could be related to the impact on the environment or to the quality of life.

When introducing new technologies, the potential benefits must be weighed up against the risks.

Sometimes unintended consequences affecting the environment can be identified. By applying the scientific method (making hypotheses, explanations and carrying out experiments), biologists can devise new ways of putting right the impact. Devising life cycle assessments helps biologists to try to minimise unintended consequences and ensure sustainability.

Some areas of biology could have a high potential risk to individuals or groups if they go wrong or if they're abused. In these areas the Government ensures that regulations are in place.

The scientific approach covers anything where data can be collected and used to test a hypothesis. It can't be used when evidence can't be collected (e.g. it can't test beliefs or values).

Just because something can be done doesn't mean that it should be done. Some areas of scientific research or the technologies resulting from them have ethical issues associated with them. This means that not all people will necessarily agree with it.

Ethical decisions have to be made, taking into account the views of everyone involved, whilst balancing the benefits and risks.

It's impossible to please everybody, so decisions are often made on the basis of which outcome will benefit most people. Within a culture there will also be some actions that are always right or wrong, no matter what the circumstances are.

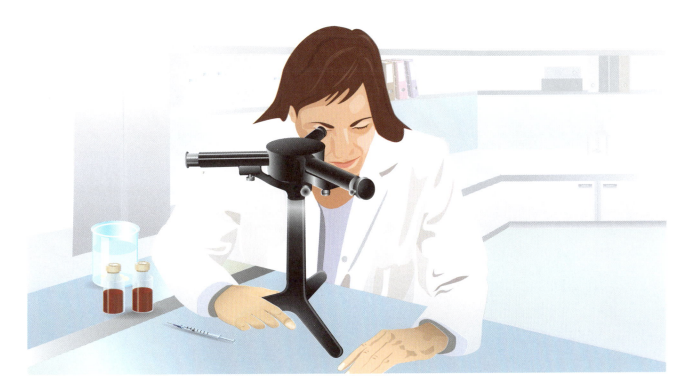

Contents

Contents

Revised

B1 You and Your Genes

Variation

Differences between individuals of the same species are called **variation**.

Variation may be due to…
- **genetic factors**, e.g. dimples, eye colour
- **environmental factors**, e.g. scars, hair style.

Genetic Causes   **Environmental Causes**

Genetic Information

Our understanding of genetics has been developed over many years by studying inheritance and **DNA** (deoxyribonucleic acid). This has allowed us to link the identification of DNA structure with the observations of changes in many organisms over time. This has led to the knowledge outlined below.

Genes carry the information needed for you to develop. **Different genes** control **different characteristics**, e.g. the colour of your hair.

Genes…
- occur in long strings called **chromosomes**
- are located inside the **nucleus** of **every cell**.

Chromosomes are made of DNA molecules. DNA molecules are…
- made up of **two very long strands**
- coiled to form a **double helix**.

DNA molecules form a complete set of instructions for…
- how the organism should be constructed
- how each cell should function.

Genes are sections of DNA. Genes **control the development** of different characteristics by **issuing instructions** to the cell. The cell carries out these instructions by producing **proteins**.

The proteins formed inside a cell can be…
- **structural proteins** (for cell growth or repair), e.g. collagen
- **functional proteins**, e.g. enzymes (to speed up chemical reactions) such as amylase.

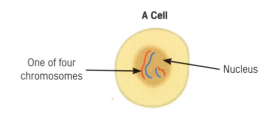

A Cell

One of four chromosomes

Nucleus

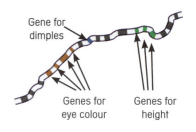

A Section of One Chromosome

Gene for dimples

Genes for eye colour

Genes for height

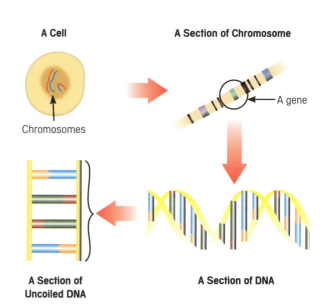

A Cell

Chromosomes

A Section of Chromosome

A gene

A Section of Uncoiled DNA

A Section of DNA

Key Words   Variation • DNA • Gene • Chromosome • Nucleus • Protein

Chromosomes

Chromosomes normally come in **pairs**:

- Both chromosomes in a pair have the **same sequence** of genes, i.e. the same genes in the same place.
- Different species have different numbers of pairs. **Human cells** contain **23 pairs** of chromosomes (46 in total).

Sex cells contain single chromosomes.

Sperm		Egg		Fertilised Egg Cell
	+		=	
23 chromosomes	+	23 chromosomes	=	46 chromosomes (23 pairs) – half from mother (egg) and half from father (sperm)

Pairs of Chromosomes in a Human Male

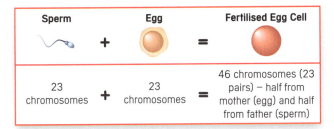

1 2 3 4 5
6 7 8 9 10 11
12 13 14 15 16 17
18 19 20 21 22 XY

Alleles

A gene can have **different versions**, called **alleles**. For example, the gene for dimples has two alleles: have dimples and have no dimples. For each gene, you inherit one allele from your father and one from your mother.

You can inherit two alleles that are the same.

HT This is called **homozygous**.

Alternatively, you can inherit two alleles that are different.

HT This is called **heterozygous**.

Brothers and sisters **randomly inherit** different combinations of alleles, which is why they can be very ditterent.

HT The combination of alleles you have is called your **genotype** and the actual characteristics you show is called your **phenotype**.

Alleles can be **dominant** or **recessive**:

- **Dominant allele** – controls the development of a characteristic, even if it's present on only one chromosome in a pair.
- **Recessive allele** – controls the development of a characteristic only if a dominant allele isn't present, i.e. if the recessive allele is present on both chromosomes in a pair.

Genetic Diagrams

Genetic diagrams (e.g. Punnett squares or family trees) are used to show all the possible combinations of alleles and outcomes for a particular gene. They use…

- **capital letters** for **dominant** alleles
- **lower case letters** for **recessive** alleles.

An example of a Punnett square is shown opposite.

Genetic Make-up of Father's Sex Cells (Have Freckles)

Genetic Make-up of Mother's Sex Cells (No Freckles)		B	B
	b	Bb	Bb
	b	Bb	Bb

Possible combinations of children (all have freckles)

B1 You and Your Genes

Genetics and Lifestyle

Most characteristics are determined by several genes working together. However, they can be influenced by **environmental factors**. For example, your height is determined by a variety of genes, but factors like diet can also affect it.

Poor diet can lead to **disease**. For example, a fatty diet can increase the risk of heart disease.

It's possible to limit the chances of getting certain diseases by making **lifestyle changes**, e.g. taking more exercise and drinking no alcohol.

Sex Chromosomes

One of the 23 pairs of **chromosomes** in a human body cell is the **sex chromosomes**:

- In **females** the sex chromosomes are **identical**; they are both **X** chromosomes.
- In **males** they are **different**; there is an **X** and a **Y** chromosome. The Y chromosome is much shorter than the X chromosome.

HT The sex of an individual is determined by a gene on the **Y chromosome** called the **sex-determining region Y** (SRY) gene.

If the gene isn't present, i.e. if there are two **X chromosomes** present, the embryo will develop into a female.

If the gene is present, i.e. if there is an X chromosome and a Y chromosome, **testes** begin to develop.

Six weeks after fertilisation, the testes start producing a hormone called **androgen**. Specialised **receptors** in the developing embryo detect the androgen and male reproductive organs begin to grow.

Sometimes the Y chromosome is present but androgen isn't detected. When this happens...

- the embryo develops female sex organs apart from the uterus
- the baby has a female body but is **infertile**.

Male

Female

X Y

X X

Half the sperm carry X chromosomes and half carry Y chromosomes.

All the eggs carry X chromosomes.

X X

X Y

If an X sperm fertilises the egg, a girl is produced.

If a Y sperm fertilises the egg, a boy is produced.

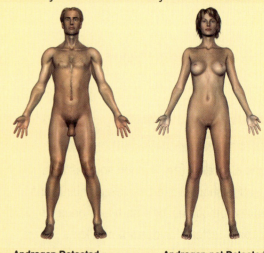

Androgen Detected
Genetically male.
Appears male.

Androgen not Detected
Genetically male.
Appears female but has no uterus.

Key Words   **Chromosome • Sex-determining region Y**

Huntington's Disease

Most characteristics are governed by a range of genes, so one 'faulty' **allele** may not affect the overall outcome. However, although rare, some disorders are caused by a single allele, e.g. **Huntington's disease**.

Huntington's disease (HD)…

- is a genetic disorder affecting the **central nervous system**. It's caused by a 'faulty' gene on the fourth pair of chromosomes
- damages the brain's **nerve cells**
- causes gradual changes, which develop into symptoms including **involuntary movement**, **clumsiness**, **memory loss**, **mood changes** and **inability to concentrate**
- is incurable, leading to premature death.

Symptoms of HD can **differ**, even within the same family. Symptoms normally develop in adulthood, which means sufferers may already have passed it on to their children. Only one parent needs to pass on the gene for a child to **inherit** it. So whether both alleles are the same or only one of the alleles is for HD, HD will develop because the allele is **dominant**.

Healthy Parent

	h	h
h	hh	hh
H	Hh	Hh

Parent with HD Gene

Each offspring has a 50% chance of inheriting the disorder

Cystic Fibrosis

Cystic fibrosis (CF) affects **cell membranes**, causing a thick, sticky mucus, especially in the **lungs**, **gut** and **pancreas**. Symptoms can include **weight loss**, **difficulty in breathing**, **chest infections** and **difficulty in digesting food**. There's no cure, but scientists have identified the allele that causes it.

Unlike Huntington's disease, the cystic fibrosis allele is **recessive**. So, if a person only possesses one allele for CF, they will have no symptoms of the disorder at all. However, they are called **carriers** because they could possibly pass on the allele to their children.

Healthy Parent

	F	F
f	Ff	Ff
F	FF	FF

Carrier Parent

Each offspring has a 50% chance of being a carrier

Carrier Parent

	F	f
f	Ff	ff
F	FF	Ff

Carrier Parent

Each offspring has a 50% chance of being a carrier and a 25% chance of inheriting the disorder

Quick Test

1. What is a chromosome?
2. What are alleles?
3. What is meant by a carrier of a genetic disease?
4. **HT** What is a phenotype?

Genetic Testing

It's possible to test a person for a faulty **allele**. If the tests are positive, an appropriate course of action must be chosen, taking into account the risks involved and the benefits that may be gained.

Testing on Adults or Children

Tests can be done to see if an adult possesses a disease-causing allele in their cells. If a positive result is obtained, the adult may choose not to have any children and, perhaps, adopt a child instead. Alternatively, the adult may still decide to have a child and accept the risk of passing on the disorder to their offspring.

Children may be tested to see if they have any disease-causing genes, so that possible preventative measures can be taken. These tests can also be carried out before prescribing certain drugs (e.g. for cancer treatment) that may have a negative effect on the individual due to their genetic make-up. In this way, more effective treatment can be undertaken.

Testing Fetuses

The fluid surrounding the **fetus** or the placenta can be tested for faulty alleles. This carries a small risk of causing a miscarriage and has other implications.

If a faulty allele is detected, the parents have to consider whether the pregnancy should be terminated and whether other family members should be told as they too may carry the faulty allele.

There are ethical concerns here, e.g. whether pregnancy termination should be considered and the possible effects the information may have on an individual or their relationships.

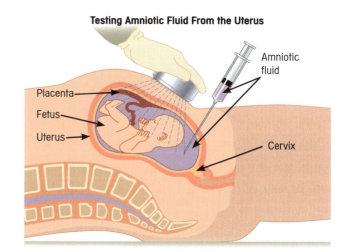

Testing Amniotic Fluid From the Uterus

Amniotic fluid

Placenta

Fetus

Uterus

Cervix

Reliability

As no test is 100% reliable, genetic testing on a fetus can have a number of outcomes, as the table opposite shows.

False negatives are rare and **false positives** even rarer. However, a false positive result means that parents may choose to terminate the pregnancy when the fetus is in fact healthy.

Counselling may also be necessary to help explain all alternative actions before a decision is made.

Outcome	Test Result	Reality
True positive	Fetus **has** the disorder	Fetus **has** the disorder
True negative	Fetus **doesn't** have the disorder	Fetus **doesn't** have the disorder
False positive	Fetus **has** the disorder	Fetus **doesn't** have the disorder
False negative	Fetus **doesn't** have the disorder	Fetus **has** the disorder

The Implications of Genetic Testing

Before genetic testing can become common practice, the following questions should be addressed:

- How can mistakes be prevented?
- Is it right to interfere with nature?
- Who has the right to decide if a disorder is worth living with?

There is always a difference between what **can** be done and what **should** be done. Governments may have the ability to test, but should they be allowed to?

Genetic testing may be used to screen individuals for…

- susceptibility to certain diseases or conditions
- possible problems with certain prescribed drugs or treatments.

It's been suggested that babies should be **screened at birth**, allowing doctors…

- to tailor healthcare and prevent problems
- to stop genetic disorders from being passed on, eliminating them completely.

One view is that this would mean less suffering and the money currently spent on treatment could be used elsewhere. The **opposing view** is that these disorders are natural and it would be wrong to eliminate them.

Storing genetic information raises questions about **confidentiality**. Should employers or insurance companies have access to this information? For example, it could be used to **discriminate** and people may be turned down for jobs or life insurance if they are found to have a **higher risk** of illness.

HT Embryo Selection

Embryo selection is another way of preventing babies from having genetic disorders. Embryos can be produced by *in vitro* **fertilisation** (IVF):

1. **Ova** are harvested from the mother and **fertilised**.
2. The embryos are tested for the faulty allele.
3. Healthy embryos are **implanted** into the **uterus**. The pregnancy proceeds as normal.

The procedure for embryo selection is called **Pre-implantation Genetic Diagnosis** (PGD):

1. After fertilisation the embryos are allowed to **divide** into eight cells before a single cell is removed from each one for testing.
2. The cells are tested to see if they carry the alleles for a **specific genetic disorder**.

Embryo selection is **controversial**:

- Some people believe it's **unnatural**.
- There are concerns that people could select certain characteristics, such as eye colour, sex, etc., in advance (pre-selection).

Pre-selection of a baby's characteristics could **reduce variation**. For example, if most people selected blue eyes for their baby, the brown eye allele could disappear in time.

Asexual Reproduction

Bacteria and other **single-cell organisms** can reproduce by dividing to form two 'new' individuals. The new individuals are **clones** (genetically identical to the parent).

This is called **asexual reproduction**. Most plants and some animals can reproduce in this way.

Variation in organisms that reproduce **asexually** is normally only caused by **environmental factors**.

Animal clones can occur naturally:

- The cells of an embryo sometimes **separate**.
- The two new embryos develop into **identical twins**.

HT Animal clones can be produced **artificially**:

- The **nucleus** from an adult body cell is transferred into an empty (nucleus removed) unfertilised egg cell.
- The new individual will have exactly the same genetic information as the donor.

There are many conflicting views on this as some people see this process as unethical. However, this technology is closely monitored and regulated by the Government.

Many plants naturally produce clones when they form **bulbs** or **runners**. Bulbs are swollen leaves that act as a store over the non-growing season. They develop into new plants in the following, and subsequent, seasons. Daffodils are an example.

Runners are stem-like outgrowths along which new plants develop. The new plants can root and grow on in the following seasons. Strawberry plants are an example.

These methods allow plants to survive and reproduce without the meeting of male and female gametes (sex cells). But, as the new plants are clones and no genetic variation is taking place, they will all be susceptible to the same diseases as the parent plant.

Cell Division During Asexual Reproduction

Parental cell with two pairs of chromosomes.

Each chromosome replicates itself.

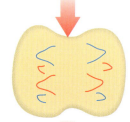

The copies are pulled apart. Cell now divides for the only time.

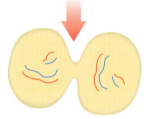

Each 'daughter' cell has the same number of chromosomes and contains the same genes as the parental cell.

Daffodils

Bulb

Strawberry Plant

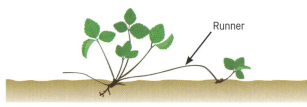

Runner

Stem Cells

Most organisms are made up of various **specialised** cells with **different structures**. In the early stages of development, cells aren't specialised. These are called **stem cells**, which will quickly develop into the many different specialised cells needed in the organism.

Stem cells have the potential to develop into any type of cell. They can potentially be used to replace damaged tissues, e.g. in patients with **Parkinson's disease**.

There are two types of stem cell:
- Adult
- Embryonic.

Adult stem cells…
- are taken from areas that are adapted for the replacement and repair of tissues, such as umbilical cord blood and bone marrow
- have the potential to develop into a range of specialised cells, but not all types.

Embryonic stem cells…
- are taken from a developing embryo, so to produce them it's necessary to clone embryos
- have the potential to develop into any kind of specialised cell.

Some people are against stem cell technology. The Government recognises that it has the potential to benefit many people, so it allows the research. However, it's tightly regulated to hopefully avoid any misuse of the process.

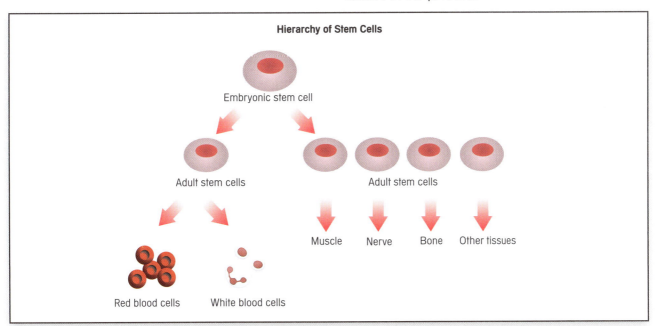

Hierarchy of Stem Cells

Embryonic stem cell

Adult stem cells

Adult stem cells

Muscle   Nerve   Bone   Other tissues

Red blood cells   White blood cells

Quick Test

1. Why will someone with only one allele for Huntington's disease definitely develop the disease?
2. Give two symptoms of cystic fibrosis.
3. Why are genetic tests carried out on fetuses?
4. What is a stem cell?
5. A stem cell taken from bone marrow is what type of stem cell?

Key Words   Stem cell • Adult stem cell • Embryonic stem cell

1 **(a)** Put a ring around the correct choice to complete the sentence. **[1]**

A gene provides instructions to make **chromosomes / proteins / nuclei / cells**.

(b) Fill in the missing word to complete the sentence. Choose from the following words: **[1]**

DNA   **pairs**   **gametes**   **alleles**

Different versions of the same gene are called ....

(c) **(i)** Complete the Punnett square below. **[4]**

Parent with Brown Eyes

	B	b
b		
B		

(Parent with Brown Eyes)

(ii) What is the chance of the offspring having brown eyes? **[1]**

....

2 Niamh is growing yeast, a single-celled fungus, in an experiment. She adds a small sample of the yeast to a growth mixture. After a few days there's more yeast in the flask than she had to start with.

Use the words below to complete the following sentences. **[2]**

asexual   **sexual**   **genetic**   **environmental**   **chromosomes**   **nucleus**   **clones**

The cells that make up Niamh's skin contain 23 pairs of ....

Yeast reproduce via .... reproduction.

All the yeast are genetically identical, therefore they're ....

The yeast don't look exactly the same. This is due to .... factors.

3 The table below is jumbled. Draw straight lines from the outcomes to the correct test results and realities. One line has been drawn for you. **[3]**

Outcome	Test Result	Reality
True positive	Fetus **has** the disorder	Fetus **doesn't** have the disorder
True negative	Fetus **has** the disorder	Fetus **has** the disorder
False positive	Fetus **doesn't** have the disorder	Fetus **has** the disorder
False negative	Fetus **doesn't** have the disorder	Fetus **doesn't** have the disorder

4 Two friends are discussing Huntington's disease.

Linda
Every pregnancy should be tested for Huntington's disease and the fetus aborted if the condition is present.

John
At least people live to middle age before the symptoms of Huntington's disease start to develop.

Write a response to Linda explaining why her idea is potentially unethical.   **[6]**

🖉 *The quality of written communication will be assessed in your answer to this question.*

5 The sex of an individual is determined by a pair of chromosomes. Males have one X and one Y chromosome; females have a pair of X chromosomes.

Explain why the **sperm** are said to 'decide' the sex of the baby.   **[3]**

HT 6 What is the meaning of **genotype**?   **[1]**

B2 Keeping Healthy

Infection

Infections are caused by microorganisms damaging body cells or producing poisons (toxins) that harm cells. Infections can be treated with drugs called **antimicrobials** (e.g. antibiotics).

Many antimicrobials kill the microorganisms but some just block or slow down their action.

HT This is called **inhibition**.

Microorganisms that cause infections include:

- **Bacteria**, e.g. bubonic plague, tuberculosis (TB) and cystitis. Treated by antibiotics.
- **Fungi**, e.g. athlete's foot, thrush and ringworm. Treated by anti-fungal medicine and antibiotics.
- **Viruses**, e.g. Asian bird flu, common cold, HIV, measles and smallpox. Very difficult to treat. Antibiotics don't work on viruses.

Microorganisms can be found on any surface, in food and drink, in water and in the air we breathe.

The body provides ideal conditions for microorganisms to grow; it's **warm**, with plenty of **nutrients** and **moisture**. Once in your body, harmful microorganisms reproduce very rapidly – some populations can double as fast as every 20 minutes.

Symptoms of an illness only show when there's a significant amount of infection. The symptoms are caused by microorganisms damaging infected cells, e.g. bursting the cells or producing harmful toxins.

The Immune Response

If microorganisms get into your body, the **immune system** is activated.

Two types of **white blood cell** play a major role in this response.

One type of white blood cell is activated when any microorganism gets into the body:

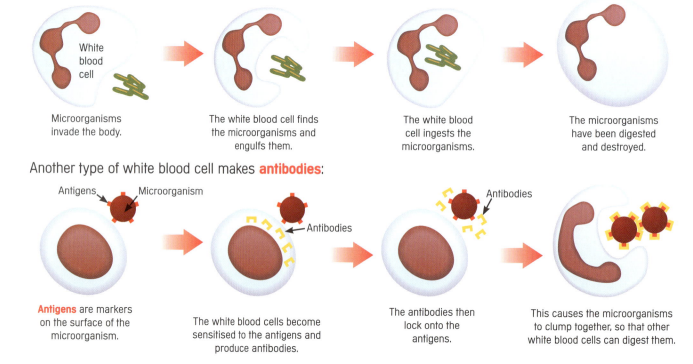

White blood cell

Microorganisms invade the body.

The white blood cell finds the microorganisms and engulfs them.

The white blood cell ingests the microorganisms.

The microorganisms have been digested and destroyed.

Another type of white blood cell makes **antibodies**:

Antigens   Microorganism

Antibodies

Antibodies

Antigens are markers on the surface of the microorganism.

The white blood cells become sensitised to the antigens and produce antibodies.

The antibodies then lock onto the antigens.

This causes the microorganisms to clump together, so that other white blood cells can digest them.

Key Words   Bacteria • Fungi • Virus • Immune system • White blood cell • Antibody • Antigen

Specialisation of Antibodies

Different microorganisms cause different diseases. Microorganisms have **unique markers**, called **antigens**, on their surface. White blood cells produce antibodies specific to the marker they need to attack.

After infection some white cells act as memory cells as they 'remember' the antigens and are able to produce antibodies quicker if the body is reinfected. This is **natural immunity** and it protects that particular individual in the future.

Example – Antibodies to Fight TB will not Fight Cholera

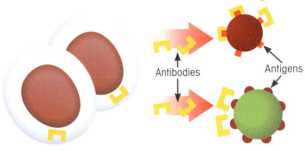

TB microorganism
Antibodies
Antigens
White blood cells
Cholera microorganism

Vaccination

A **vaccination** helps the body to develop **immunity** and produce **specific** antibodies and memory cells so that microorganisms can be destroyed before they **cause infection**. Vaccinations are never completely safe and can produce side effects, most of which are minor like rashes. **Extreme side effects** are **rare**, but the vaccination usually carries less risk than the disease. However, because of genetic variation, some people may be affected more than others. But the benefits to the majority are usually considered greater than the risks, so this course of action is often recommended by the Government.

Some vaccines have to be redeveloped regularly because microorganisms mutate (randomly genetically change) to produce **new varieties** (**strains**). For example, flu vaccinations are **renewed every year** because new strains appear.

1 A weakened/dead strain of the microorganism is injected. Antigens on the modified microorganism's surface cause the white blood cells to produce specific antibodies.

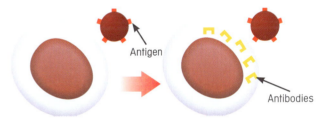

Antigen
Antibodies

2 The white blood cells that are capable of quickly producing the specific antibody remain in the bloodstream.

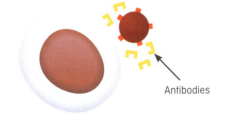

Antibodies

Growth of Microorganisms

Microorganisms can reproduce extremely quickly. The graph shows how the population of a bacterium that reproduces every 30 minutes increases, beginning with a very small number and reaching more than 10 000 in only five hours.

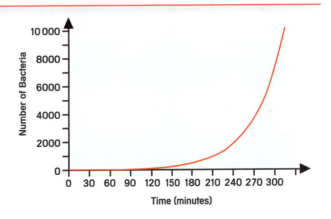

B2 Keeping Healthy

Choices

People can refuse to have a vaccination. But the more who say no, the greater the chance of a **disease outbreak** (epidemic) and the **faster** it will spread.

HT It's important to vaccinate as many people as possible to prevent epidemics like measles. If **more** than 95% of the population are vaccinated then the unvaccinated will be protected too, as the risk of contact with an infected person is **small**. If the percentage drops **below** 95%, then there's a greater chance of contact with infected people.

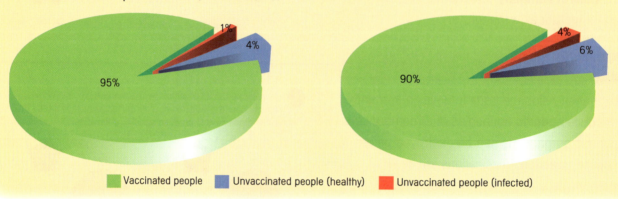

1%
4%
95%

4%
6%
90%

■ Vaccinated people ■ Unvaccinated people (healthy) ■ Unvaccinated people (infected)

Resistance to Antimicrobials

Over time bacteria and fungi can become **resistant** to **antimicrobials**.

HT **Random mutations** can occur in the genes of microorganisms:

- **New strains** develop.
- These are less affected by antimicrobials, so they can **reproduce** and **pass on** their resistance.

As varieties of bacteria and fungi become resistant, there are **fewer ways** to defeat them.

There's growing concern that microorganisms that are resistant to all drugs will develop (i.e. superbugs). In the UK, diseases such as MRSA (Methicillin-resistant Staphylococcus aureus) have a high degree of drug resistance.

To help prevent antimicrobial resistance…

- doctors should only prescribe them when **completely necessary**
- patients should always **complete the course**.

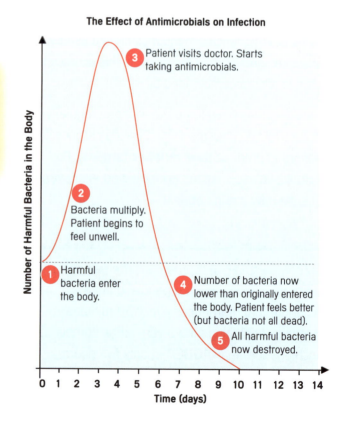

The Effect of Antimicrobials on Infection

Number of Harmful Bacteria in the Body

3 Patient visits doctor. Starts taking antimicrobials.

2 Bacteria multiply. Patient begins to feel unwell.

1 Harmful bacteria enter the body.

4 Number of bacteria now lower than originally entered the body. Patient feels better (but bacteria not all dead).

5 All harmful bacteria now destroyed.

0 1 2 3 4 5 6 7 8 9 10 11 12 13 14
Time (days)

Testing New Drugs

New drugs are tested for **safety** and **effectiveness** before they can be used. The methods used are often controversial.

Tests on Human Cells Grown in the Laboratory	Tests on Animals
Advantages • Show if drugs are effective. • Show if drugs will damage cells. • No people or animals are harmed. **Disadvantages** • Don't show effects on whole organism. • Some say growing human cells is wrong.	**Advantages** • Show if drugs are effective within body conditions. • Show if drugs are safe for whole body. **Disadvantages** • Animals can suffer and die. • Animals may react differently to humans.

Clinical Trials

Clinical trials are carried out on…
- **healthy volunteers** to test for safety
- people with the **illness** to test for safety and effectiveness.

Placebos (or harmless drugs) are used in comparison trials. Using placebos means that the patient **isn't** treated for the problem – can this be a good thing?

(HT) Clinical trials compare the effects of **new** and **old** drugs.

Blind trials – Patients **don't know** which drugs they're given but the doctor **does**. If the patient knows, they may give biased information. It's possible the doctor's body language may give clues.

Double-blind trials – Neither patient nor doctor know which drug is used. Results should be very accurate, due to removing bias. Sometimes it's impossible to keep what the drug is from the doctor, e.g. if the patient says the new drug has a different taste.

Open-label trials – Both the doctor and patient know that they are using a new treatment. This is used when the new treatment is very similar to the original, or when a drug is being compared to physical therapy.

Long-term trials – These are important for ensuring that there are no harmful side effects and to make sure that the treatment continues to be effective.

Quick Test

1. What type of microorganism can't be treated with antibiotics?
2. Which three conditions are ideally needed for microorganisms to grow rapidly?
3. Which type of blood cell 'fights' microorganisms?
4. What are the unique markers on the cell surface of a microorganism called?
5. Why are microorganisms like MRSA often called 'superbugs'?

B2 Keeping Healthy

The Heart

The heart…
- is a **double pump** as it pumps blood from its right side to the lungs and pumps blood from its left side to the rest of the body
- pumps blood to provide the body cells with **nutrients** and **oxygen**, and to **remove waste products**
- is made up of **muscle cells** that need a blood supply from the **coronary artery** to function properly.

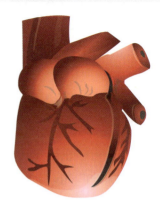

Blood Vessels

The main blood vessels are arteries, veins and capillaries. Their structure is related to their function.

Arteries carry blood away from the heart **towards** the organs. Substances from the blood can't pass through artery walls.

An artery has a thick, elastic, muscular wall to cope with the high pressure in the vessel.

Veins carry blood from the organs **back** to the heart. Substances can't pass through the veins' walls.

A vein has a thinner wall than an artery and has less elastic muscular fibre due to the lower pressure in the vessel.

Veins have pocket valves along their length to keep blood flowing in the right direction.

Capillaries are very narrow vessels that carry blood between arteries and veins, and through the organs. They have walls made of a single layer of cells. It's here that substances are exchanged between blood and body cells.

Artery

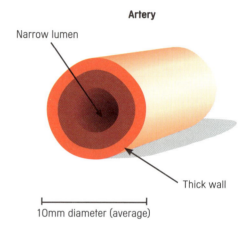

Narrow lumen

Thick wall

10mm diameter (average)

Vein

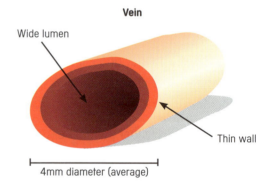

Wide lumen

Thin wall

4mm diameter (average)

Capillary

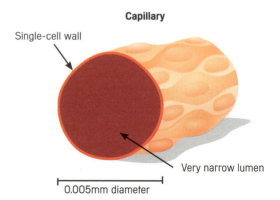

Single-cell wall

Very narrow lumen

0.005mm diameter

Heart Disease

Heart disease…

- is a **structural** or **functional** abnormality that can lead to a heart attack
- is usually caused by **lifestyle** and/or **genetic** factors. It's **not** caused by infection.

Lifestyle factors that can lead to heart disease include poor diet, smoking and stress. Misuse of drugs like Ecstasy, cannabis and alcohol can affect the heart rate (pulse rate) and blood pressure, increasing the risk of a heart attack.

A heart attack occurs when **fatty deposits** build up in blood vessels supplying the heart. Blood flow is restricted and the muscle cells in the heart don't get enough oxygen and nutrients.

Heart disease is more **common** in the UK than in non-industrialised countries due to lifestyle differences in their populations.

Precautions Against Heart Disease

Precautions people can take against heart disease include…

- regular exercise, e.g. 20 minutes brisk walking every day
- not smoking
- maintaining a healthy weight and reducing salt intake.

Blood Pressure

Heart rate (pulse rate) and blood pressure measurements can be used to monitor the risk of heart disease. Blood pressure is given in two numbers:

- A higher number (obtained when the heart is contracting).
- A lower number (obtained when the heart is relaxing).

All measurements that are regarded as 'normal' are given within a range because people vary in height, weight, etc.

High measurements can indicate a high risk of heart disease. Studies of the population using **genetic** and **epidemiological** information can be used to identify lifestyle factors that contribute to heart disease.

Pulse Rate Being Taken

Blood Pressure Being Taken

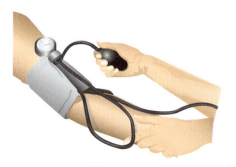

Water Balance

Water is **input** (gained) from…
- food and drinks
- respiration.

Water is **output** (lost) through…
- sweating
- breathing
- excretion of faeces and urine.

Your body has to **balance** these different inputs and outputs to ensure that there's enough water inside cells for cell activity to take place.

The kidneys play a vital role in balancing water, waste and other chemicals in the blood.

Both hormonal and nervous systems are involved in maintaining the stability of the internal environment of the body. This process is called **homeostasis**.

All the body's automatic control systems need to keep a variety of factors within a safe range to allow them to work properly. For example:

1. Water levels are monitored by receptor cells in the brain.
2. The brain then processes this information and coordinates the response to the **effector** organ.
3. The **pituitary gland** is an effector which produces the response.
4. This results in a **hormone** being released to affect the kidneys and the amount of water that's released or retained in the blood.

Regulating Water Levels

Your kidneys balance the water level in your body:
- When the water level is **too high**, your kidneys reabsorb less water and a **large amount of dilute urine** is produced.
- When the water level is **too low**, your kidneys reabsorb more water and a **small amount of concentrated urine** is produced.

The amount of water that needs to be reabsorbed into the blood plasma depends on…
- the external temperature
- the amount of exercise taken
- the fluid intake.

Alcohol causes a large amount of dilute urine to be produced, which can adversely affect overall health. This can lead to **dehydration**.

Ecstasy causes a small amount of less dilute urine to be produced.

🔴HT Anti-diuretic Hormone

The concentration of urine is controlled by a hormone called **anti-diuretic hormone** (**ADH**), which is released into your blood via the **pituitary gland**.

Controlling water balance is an example of **negative feedback**, where one system is the reverse to another in order to maintain a steady state.

When your blood water level becomes **too high** (i.e. there's too much water), the following happens:

1 **Receptors** in your **hypothalamus** detect a **decrease** in salt concentration. No stimulus is sent to the pituitary gland.

2 **Less** ADH is secreted into the blood.

3 Your kidneys become **less permeable**, so less water is reabsorbed.

4 Your bladder fills with a **large quantity of dilute urine**.

If your blood water level becomes **too low** (i.e. not enough water), the opposite happens:

1 Receptors in your **hypothalamus** detect an increase in salt concentration. A stimulus is sent to the pituitary gland. **Thirst** is stimulated to encourage drinking.

2 **More** ADH is secreted into the blood.

3 Your kidneys become **more permeable**, so more water is reabsorbed.

4 Your bladder fills with a small quantity of **concentrated urine**.

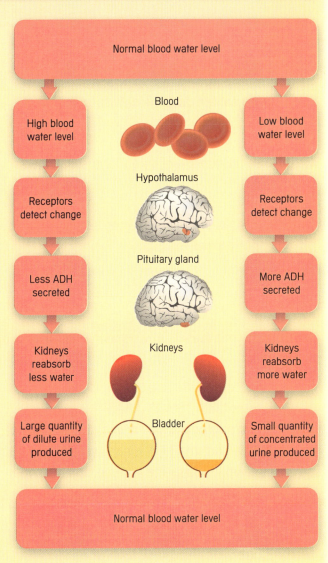

ADH and Drugs

Drugs such as alcohol and Ecstasy affect the production of ADH in different ways:

• **Alcohol** causes ADH to be **suppressed**, so more water leaves the body in the urine.

• **Ecstasy** causes **too much** ADH to be produced, so too much water remains in the blood. Osmosis then causes the water to leave the blood, causing brain cells to swell and burst.

Quick Test

1 Why is the heart called a double pump?
2 What is measured by the higher number in a blood pressure reading?
3 What is the name of the process that maintains the internal conditions in the body?

1 The table below shows the recorded number of alcohol-related deaths per year in a European country.

Year	2001	2002	2003	2004	2005	2006
Men	3576	3632	3970	3016	4096	4272
Women	1900	1951	2011	2114	2412	2245

(a) What pattern does the data show for the six-year period in general? [1]

....

(b) Give an example of an outlier result in the above data. [1]

....

(c) The table only refers to alcohol-related deaths. Suggest **two** other lifestyle factors that are likely to cause premature death. [2]

....

....

(d) Suggest a reason why someone can dispute the data based on the table above. [1]

....

....

2 (a) These steps describe the four stages that take place when white blood cells attack a foreign microorganism. They're in the wrong order. Put the steps in the correct order by writing the letters in the empty boxes. One has been done for you. [2]

    A Microorganisms are ingested by the white blood cell.

    B Microorganisms are detected by the body.

    C Microorganisms are completely digested and destroyed.

    D White blood cell surrounds the microorganism.

    (**B** | | |)

(b) Label the diagram below, which shows how the body fights infection. [4]

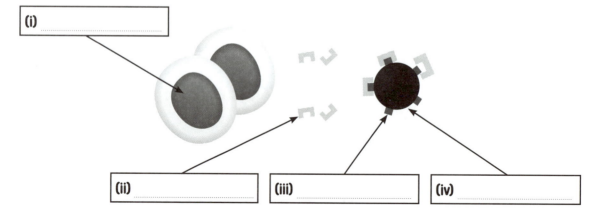

(i) ....

(ii) ....

(iii) ....

(iv) ....

3 **(a)** Vaccines prevent disease. What is contained in a vaccine? Put a tick (✓) in the box next to the correct answer. **[1]**

Antibiotics ☐

A weakened or dead strain of the disease-causing microorganism ☐

An active strain of the disease-causing microorganism ☐

Antibodies ☐

(b) **(i)** Why can vaccines never be completely safe? **[1]**

(ii) Why do new vaccines have to be developed regularly for diseases such as flu? **[1]**

4 This question is about testing a new drug.

In each part below, put a ring around the correct word or phrase.

(a) In a trial to test a new drug it was found that, in most cases, the test sample of patients who had been ill had shown a marked improvement in their condition after a course of treatment.

(i) We can say that this shows a **correlation** / **relationship** between the treatment and its effect. **[1]**

(ii) From the information above, the drug **definitely causes** / **possibly does not cause** the outcome effect. **[1]**

(b) A second group of patients was given a placebo in place of the drug. No members of this group showed any improvement in their condition.

(i) A placebo is **a similar drug** / **a harmless drug**. **[1]**

(ii) Using all the information in this question, it can be said that it is highly likely that the drug **causes** / **does not cause** the outcome effect. **[1]**

HT **5** In the winter, we urinate more because we don't lose water in sweating. The blood water level gets very high. Explain how this is brought about in the body. **[3]**

B3 Life on Earth

Adaptation to the Environment

A particular **species** (similar organisms that are capable of breeding together to produce fertile offspring) is adapted to its environment, which helps it to survive and increase its chances of reproducing. For example, a cactus is adapted to a desert environment by having…

- its leaves reduced to spines to cut down water loss
- a thick outer layer to cut down water loss
- a deep, wide-spreading root system to obtain as much water as possible.

A fish is adapted to live in water by having…

- gills to take oxygen from water rather than air
- a streamlined shape and fins to move easily through water
- a swim bladder (an air-filled sac) to help it maintain position in water.

A species may become extinct if it can't adapt to changes such as…

- increased **competition**
- new **predators**
- new **diseases**.

Food Chains

Organisms don't live in isolation. Different species of animals or plants compete for resources in the same habitat.

Food chains can show the feeding relationships between organisms. When animals eat plants or other animals, energy is passed up the food chain.

Animals are dependent upon each other and their environment for survival.

For example, if rabbits became extinct, then the stoat and the fox might be at risk. Their numbers might then be reduced as competition for food increased.

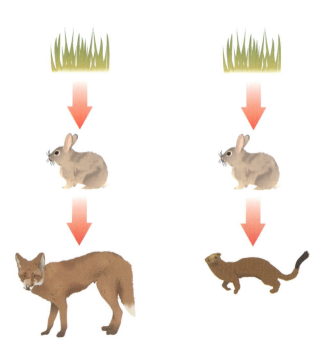

Food Webs

Food webs…

- show how all the food chains in a habitat are **inter-related**
- can be complicated as many animals have **varied** diets
- **(HT)** show how all the living organisms are dependent on each other (**interdependence**).

Environmental changes can alter the food web. For example, less rain could reduce the amount of lettuce and cause reductions in slug numbers.

If the changes are too great, organisms will die before they can reproduce, eventually becoming extinct.

Food Web

Top Carnivore — Hawk, Fox, Barn Owl

2nd Consumer — Blue Tit, Mistle Thrush

1st Consumer — Bee, Greenfly, Slug, Rabbit, Chaffinch, Dormouse

Producers — Rose, Lettuce, Grass, Barley

Energy Transfer

All living things on Earth ultimately get their **energy** from the Sun. The energy is transferred in the following ways:

- Plants **absorb** a small proportion of the Sun's energy during **photosynthesis**. They store the energy in the chemicals (e.g. starch, cellulose) that make up their cells.
- Energy is **transferred** to other organisms when plants and animals are **eaten** or **decompose**.
- Energy is also transferred when **decay** organisms feed off dead organisms and the waste products of animals.

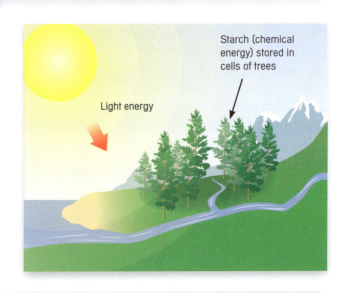

Light energy

Starch (chemical energy) stored in cells of trees

B3 Life on Earth

Ecosystems and Energy Transfer

An **ecosystem** (e.g. a pond or a wood) is an area containing a self-sustained community of organisms and their physical surroundings (e.g. soil type, climate, etc.).

Within an ecosystem there are…

- **autotrophs** (self-feeders), for example, plants that make their own food. They are also known as **producers**.
- **heterotrophs**, for example, animals and decay organisms that are unable to make their own food so they get their energy by **consuming** other organisms.

Heterotrophs that eat plants are called **herbivores**. They are **primary consumers**.

Heterotrophs that eat other animals are called **carnivores**. They are **secondary** or **tertiary consumers**.

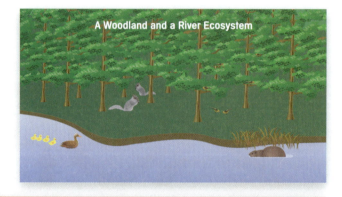

A Woodland and a River Ecosystem

Energy in Food Chains

Energy in a food chain always flows in one direction:
1. Light energy flows from the **Sun**.
2. The light energy is transferred to an **autotroph**, which captures the energy, uses it for photosynthesis and stores it in its cells.
3. A **herbivore heterotroph** eats the autotroph. Some energy stored in the plant is transferred and stored in the herbivore's cells.
4. A **carnivore heterotroph** eats the herbivore heterotroph. Some energy is transferred to the carnivore and stored in its cells.
5. Dead organisms are fed on by decay organisms (**decomposers**, e.g. bacteria and fungi).

HT Dead organisms are also fed on by **detritivores** (e.g. woodlice that can re-enter the food chain).

At each stage of the food chain, a large proportion of energy is…
- lost through heat or respiration
- excreted as waste products
- trapped in materials such as bone and fur.

This means **less energy** is available at each stage of energy transfer, which means there's a **limit** to the length of a food chain.

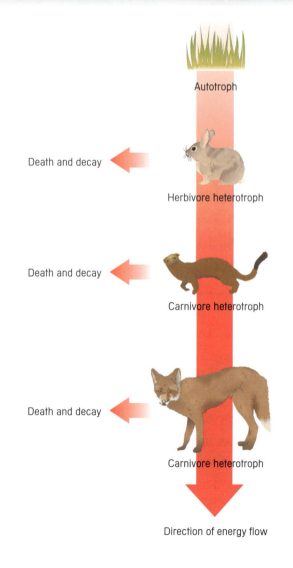

Autotroph

Death and decay

Herbivore heterotroph

Death and decay

Carnivore heterotroph

Death and decay

Carnivore heterotroph

Direction of energy flow

Key Words   Ecosystem • Autotroph • Heterotroph • Herbivore • Carnivore • Decomposer • Detritivore

Calculating Energy Efficiency

You can calculate the **energy efficiency** at each stage of a food chain using this formula:

$$\text{Percentage of energy transferred} = \frac{\text{Input energy}}{\text{Output energy}} \times 100$$

Example

This arrow diagram shows the feeding relationship between a green plant, a caterpillar and a bird. Calculate how efficient the energy transfer is for the caterpillar feeding on the plant.

$$\text{Percentage of energy transferred} = \frac{\text{Input energy}}{\text{Output energy}} \times 100$$

$$= \frac{80}{800} \times 100 = \mathbf{10\%}$$

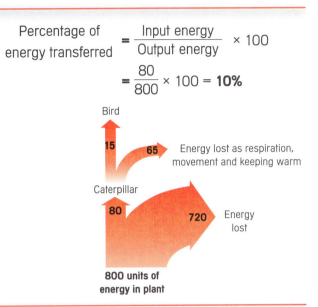

Bird

15   65   Energy lost as respiration, movement and keeping warm

Caterpillar

80   720   Energy lost

800 units of energy in plant

Cycles in Nature

All materials (e.g. nitrogen and carbon) are **recycled** in the natural world. As energy can't be created or destroyed (it can only be changed in type), it can't be recycled.

Energy is always eventually lost from the system, so a constant input is needed (from the Sun).

The Nitrogen Cycle

Nitrogen is recycled in the following way:

- Animals get nitrogen by eating protein in other plants or animals.
- Excess nitrogen is removed by **excretion**, e.g. as **urea** in urine.
- After death, plants and animals are **decomposed** by decay organisms, e.g. **bacteria** and **fungi**, breaking down protein into nitrogen compounds such as nitrates.

HT These are the other stages in the nitrogen cycle:

- Nitrogen in the air can be removed (**fixed**) by **nitrogen-fixing** bacteria found in the soil and in the root nodules of plants like clover and beans (**leguminous** plants). The nitrogen is then converted into compounds, e.g. nitrates.
- Nitrates are taken up by plant roots and converted to **protein**.
- Nitrates can be broken down into nitrogen by bacteria in the soil in a process called **denitrification**.

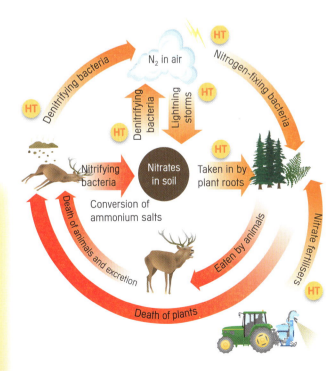

Denitrifying bacteria

N_2 in air

HT

Nitrogen-fixing bacteria

Denitrifying bacteria

Lightning storms

HT

HT

HT

Nitrifying bacteria

Nitrates in soil

Taken in by plant roots

Conversion of ammonium salts

Death of animals and excretion

Eaten by animals

Nitrate fertilisers

HT

Death of plants

B3 Life on Earth

The Carbon Cycle

Carbon is recycled in the following way:

- Carbon dioxide in the air is removed by plants in **photosynthesis** and is incorporated into their cells.
- Animals eat protein (other plants or animals) and use the carbon in their cells.
- Plants and animals **respire**, releasing waste carbon dioxide into the air.
- **Combustion** (burning) in forest fires and combustion of **fossil fuels** (e.g. oil, coal and gas) releases carbon dioxide into the air.
- Decomposer organisms, like bacteria and fungi, break down dead material and waste products, and release carbon dioxide into the atmosphere.

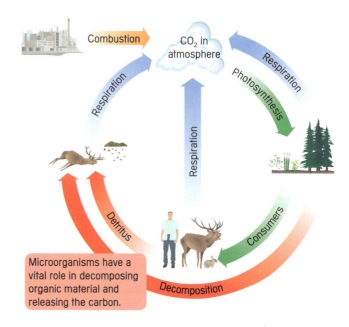

Microorganisms have a vital role in decomposing organic material and releasing the carbon.

Measuring Environmental Change

All living and non-living data can be interpreted together to investigate how the environment is changing (or not). This data can be obtained in the following ways:

- Using meters to measure levels of oxygen, carbon dioxide, nitrates and temperature, etc.
- Using living organisms as **indicators**. For example, mayfly larvae in rivers need high oxygen levels. **Pollution** reduces the amount of oxygen so, if mayfly larvae are found in significant numbers, the level of pollution in the river water is fairly low. Other living indicator organisms include **lichens** (which don't grow if the air is polluted) and **phytoplankton** (the plants found in plankton).

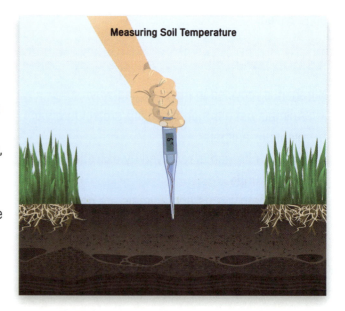

Measuring Soil Temperature

Quick Test

1. What is meant by a species?
2. How are cactus leaves adapted to reduce water loss by evaporation?
3. What does a food chain show?
4. What is the ultimate source of energy for the Earth?
5. What is a heterotroph?
6. HT What do detritivores feed on?

Combustion • Indicator organism • Pollution

Life on Earth

Life on Earth began about **3500 million** years ago.

During that time there has been a large number of species living on Earth, many of which are now **extinct**.

A species is a group of organisms that can freely breed with each other to produce fertile offspring.

The very first living things developed from **simple molecules** that could **copy** or **replicate** themselves.

It's not known whether these molecules…

- were produced by conditions on Earth at the time (harsh surface conditions, or in deep sea vents), or
- arrived on Earth from an external source, e.g. a comet hitting Earth.

Experiments have simulated the harsh conditions on Earth millions of years ago, which led to **simple organic molecules** developing.

There's evidence of **simple organic molecules** existing in gas clouds in space and in comets.

Timescale of the Earth

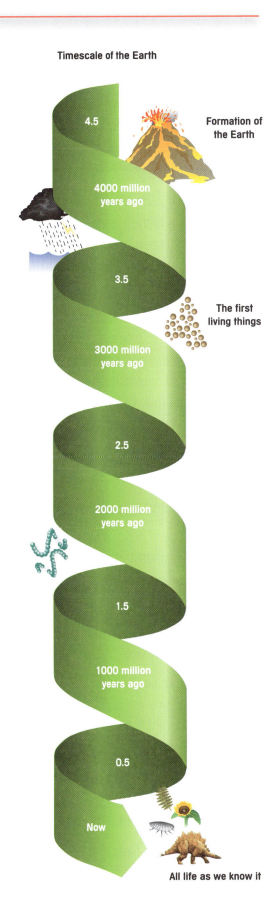

4.5 — Formation of the Earth

4000 million years ago

3.5 — The first living things

3000 million years ago

2.5

2000 million years ago

1.5

1000 million years ago

0.5

Now — All life as we know it

B3 Life on Earth

The Beginning of Life

Evidence suggests that all existing organisms share certain traits, including **cellular structure** and the **genetic** code, **DNA**. This would mean that all existing organisms share a **common ancestor** and evolved from very simple living things. Two sources of evidence support this: the **fossil** record and DNA evidence.

The Fossil Record

Fossil evidence supports the common ancestor theory and shows the history of species and the evolutionary changes over millions of years.

Fossils can be formed from the…

- hard parts of organisms that don't decay easily
- parts of animals and plants that haven't decayed because one or more of the conditions needed for decay were absent, e.g. oxygen or moisture
- soft parts of organisms that can be replaced by minerals as they decay. This can preserve traces of footprints or burrows.

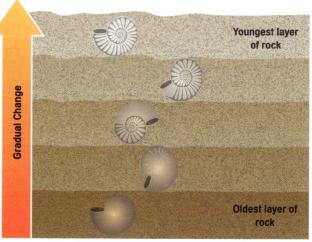

Evolution of Ammonites

Gradual Change →

Youngest layer of rock

Oldest layer of rock

*Ammonites were early sea creatures.

DNA Evidence

DNA evidence also supports the common ancestor theory. Analysing **DNA** of both living organisms and fossils shows the similarities and the differences.

This can be used to fill gaps in the **fossil record**. The more shared genes organisms have, the more closely related they are.

Comparing **gene sequences** reveals that the DNA of some organisms is very similar to organisms that seem very different.

For example, human DNA shares 98.8% of chimpanzee DNA, our nearest genetic relative. A mouse, which appears very dissimilar from humans, shares 85% of chimpanzee DNA.

Evolution by natural selection made life as it is today. If conditions on Earth had been different, then the results could have been very different.

Mouse   Chimpanzee   Human

Key Words   DNA • Common ancestor • Fossil

Evolution by Natural Selection

Evolution…

- is the slow, continual change over many generations
- may result in a new species that is **better adapted** to its environment (and the extinction of others).

In the 1830s, Charles Darwin created a testable **theory of evolution**, studying life on the Galapagos Islands, including the different types of finch.

Darwin's theory of evolution by **natural selection** was based around four key points:

1. Individuals show **variation**, i.e. differences due to their genes.
2. There's **competition** for food and mates. Also, disease and predators keep population sizes constant in spite of many offspring.
3. Those better adapted are more likely to survive and reproduce while others die out. This is '**survival of the fittest**'.
4. Survivors pass on genes to their offspring, resulting in an improved organism evolving over generations.

Darwin linked all these observations and deduced that the **best adapted** organisms would **survive** and **reproduce**. This natural selection relies on variation caused by the genes and the environment. However, only genetic variation, usually caused by **mutation**, can be passed on, and only then if it has occurred in the sex cells. **Environmental variation**, such as the loss of a finger, can't be passed on.

Another scientist working in the early 1800s, Jean-Baptiste Lamarck, had a theory that evolution was caused by a force in the environment. This caused organisms to change to suit the environment.

Many believed in this idea but today Darwin's theory is much more widely accepted as it fits with our recent understanding of genes, whereas Lamarck's theory doesn't. Darwin's original theory has been supported by many other scientists repeating and peer reviewing his observations.

Genetic mutations and environmental changes allow the natural selection due to competition, and subsequent reproduction and isolation within a particular habitat, to lead to evolution. However, scientists can't ever be certain of how life began; evidence is incomplete, new discoveries are being made and theories can change according to the known evidence.

Example of Change

Peppered moths are naturally pale and speckled, so are well camouflaged against silver birch trees.

However, during the Industrial Revolution, air pollution discoloured the trees with soot and natural selection led to a **new variety** of peppered moth:

1. **Variation** – some moths were naturally darker due to their genes.
2. **Competition** – darker-coloured and paler moths had to compete for food.
3. **Better adapted** – darker moths were better camouflaged against the blackened trees and buildings. Paler moths were seen by birds and were eaten.
4. **Passing on genes** – darker moths were more likely to survive and breed, passing on their genes for darker pigmentation.

The Clean Air Act reduced air pollution, which meant more silver birch trees stayed 'silver'. This gave the pale variety an advantage so numbers began to grow again. Today, the presence of the pale variety is regarded as a clean air marker.

Dark Peppered Moth

Pale Peppered Moth

Selective Breeding

Selective breeding is when animals with certain traits are mated to produce offspring with certain desirable characteristics. Selective breeding can produce two outcomes:

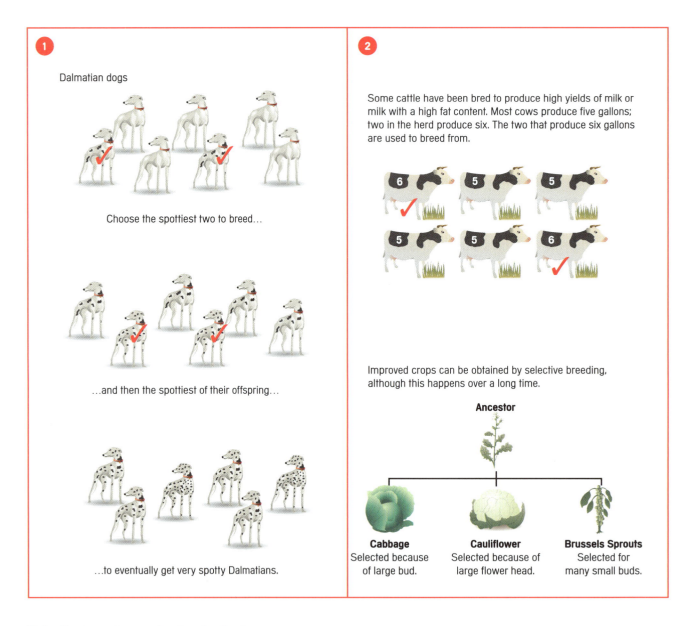

1

Dalmatian dogs

Choose the spottiest two to breed…

…and then the spottiest of their offspring…

…to eventually get very spotty Dalmatians.

2

Some cattle have been bred to produce high yields of milk or milk with a high fat content. Most cows produce five gallons; two in the herd produce six. The two that produce six gallons are used to breed from.

Improved crops can be obtained by selective breeding, although this happens over a long time.

Ancestor

Cabbage
Selected because of large bud.

Cauliflower
Selected because of large flower head.

Brussels Sprouts
Selected for many small buds.

Selective breeding and natural selection are very similar, but one is natural and the other is carried out by humans for their own purposes, not to suit the environment.

Negative Effects of Human Activity

The rate of **extinction** of species is increasing, mainly due to humans, and this may reduce biodiversity and reduce sustainability. Examples include...

- the introduction of new predators or competition, e.g. mitten crabs travelled in ships to the UK, where they ate native species of crab
- industrial activities causing global warming
- deforestation clears areas, increases carbon dioxide levels and alters the carbon cycle.

Extinctions Caused Directly by Man

The **Great Auk** (a sea bird)...

- only laid one egg a year and couldn't fly, so was vulnerable
- was hunted for food and its feathers. The last pair was killed in 1844.

The **smallpox** virus...

- was eradicated deliberately by man by mass vaccination
- was declared extinct in nature in 1980. The only examples are stored in two laboratories.

Extinctions Caused Indirectly by Man

The **Rodrigues pigeon**...

- was native to Rodrigues Island in the Indian Ocean
- became extinct when ships visiting the island accidentally introduced rats, which preyed on the birds.

The **Gould's Mouse**...

- disappeared rapidly after Europeans settled in Australia – they were affected by changes to their habitat
- was thought to have been hunted by cats and killed by diseases from rats and mice (which were introduced by man).

B3 Life on Earth

Maintaining Biodiversity

The term **biodiversity** means the variety of life that exists on Earth. This refers to the many varieties of species and also to the genetic variation of individuals within species.

Every time a species becomes extinct, information stored in its genetic code is **lost**.

Projects like the Kew Gardens Millennium Seed Bank Project prevent genetic codes being lost by collecting and storing seeds from all over the world.

Extinctions mean **less variety** on Earth. Without variety people would start to run out of food crops and medicines. Many medicines are developed from plants or animals. There are potentially many medicines in areas like the Amazon rainforest – an area rapidly undergoing deforestation.

By understanding how our actions can impact on biodiversity, scientists hope to discover ways to use the Earth's resources in a sustainable way.

Classification of Life

As life is so diverse, all living things have been classified into groups based on their similarities and differences in their physical appearance and DNA.

Life is divided into large groups, **kingdoms**, e.g. animals and plants, containing many organisms with only a few things in common.

Each kingdom is then subdivided into smaller groups containing fewer organisms with more in common with each other. The smallest of these groups is called **species**.

Humans are in…
- the kingdom **Animals** (Latin *Animalia*)
- the species **Modern Man** (Latin *Homo sapiens*).

Hamsters are in…
- the kingdom **Animals** (Latin *Animalia*)
- the species **Golden hamster** (Latin *Mesocritecus aureus*).

Sustaining Biodiversity

Sustainability means that the needs and requirements of people are met **without damaging** the Earth for future generations. Conserving all species of living things to maintain biodiversity is a key part of this process.

Huge fields of a single crop (monoculture) don't help to maintain biodiversity because they don't provide a base for many food chains or different habitats to support a variety of species. Smaller fields, separated by hedgerows and growing a variety of crops, may be a possible answer. However, commercial viability has to be considered.

Allowing 'weed' plants to grow (organic growing), rather than using herbicides and pesticides, may help to maintain biodiversity. However, this might mean reduced yields and more expensive food. The question is whether we can afford this economically or commercially.

Packaging and Sustainability

Companies and individuals often use a lot of packaging for food and goods, most of which ends up in landfill sites, where it remains for many years. We are running out of space and need alternatives.

The following are helping to reduce the amount of packaging that goes to landfill:

- Household and community waste-recycling schemes.
- Using packaging made from **biodegradable** materials instead of oil-based plastics.

Examples of the use of biodegradable packaging include the following:

- Using cardboard instead of polystyrene as packaging in parcels. Cardboard breaks down relatively quickly or can be recycled.
- Making carrier bags from cellulose extracted from plants such as potatoes. This makes the bags biodegradable and improves sustainability as it reduces oil usage.

Although we can use alternative materials, the best option is to reduce the amount of packaging altogether. Reasons for this include the following:

- Any material that's used requires energy to make it, so by not using it there are energy and cost savings.
- Transport costs can be reduced because less packaging means goods weigh less and take up less room. In turn, less transport means less pollution.

Anything that's discarded in a landfill site takes time to break down, even if it's made of a biodegradable material. The reason is that there isn't enough oxygen available for the decomposer organisms to function efficiently in the tightly-packed site.

An Example of Household Recycling

GLASS

Heavily Packaged Egg

Lightly Packaged Egg

Quick Test

1. What process removes carbon dioxide from the air?
2. What is natural selection?
3. Name the scientist who suggested the theory of natural selection.
4. What is meant by 'sustainability'?
5. **HT** What do nitrogen-fixing bacteria do?
6. **HT** What process in bacteria breaks down nitrates to nitrogen?

1. Polar bears are adapted to live on the ice in the extremely cold Arctic area around the North Pole.

A polar bear…
- has white, very thick fur, with a thick layer of fat under its skin, small ears and nose
- has very sharp teeth and strong jaws
- has large, rough skinned paws with curved claws
- feeds mainly on seals.

Use this information to explain how the polar bear is adapted to survive in the Arctic. **[6]**

✐ *The quality of written communication will be assessed in your answer to this question.*

2. Look at the information in the table below.

Distance to Town Centre (km)	0	2	4	6	8	10
Number of Different Lichen Species	0	2	9	32	54	61
Sulfur Dioxide Levels (arbitrary units)	185	140	90	34	8	0

(a) What is the relationship between the number of lichen species and the level of sulfur dioxide? **[1]**

(b) Suggest a reason, based on these figures, why someone may argue with your answer to (a). **[1]**

(c) The number of lichens could be used to monitor sulfur dioxide levels in the area. Organisms like this are given what name? **[1]**

(d) Suggest one reason why the sulfur dioxide levels change as the distance from the town centre increases. **[1]**

3 Which of the following are **heterotrophs** and which are **autotrophs**? Write an **H** in the box for a heterotroph and an **A** for an autotroph. [3]

Cabbage	
Human	
Elm tree	

Shark	
Ant	
Orchid	

4 (a) Give **three** reasons why a species may become extinct. [3]

....

....

....

(b) Genetic variation may allow some species to avoid extinction. How might genetic changes occur? [1]

....

5 This diagram shows the energy flow through a grassland habitat in one year.

(a) What process in grass absorbs the energy from the Sun? [1]

....

(b) Calculate the difference between the energy absorbed by the grass and the energy passed from the grass to other living things. [1]

....

(c) Calculate the efficiency of energy transfer from sheep to humans in the above diagram. [2]

....

....

HT 6 In the nitrogen cycle, what is the importance of...

(a) nitrogen fixation? [1]

....

(b) denitrification? [1]

....

B4 The Processes of Life

Cells

Cells are the building blocks of all living things.

All cells contain…

- **DNA**
- **organelles**.

DNA molecules are in the form of a **double helix** and contain the genetic code.

Organelles are the different parts of the cell's structure. They do different jobs within the cell and work together to allow the cell to perform a specific function.

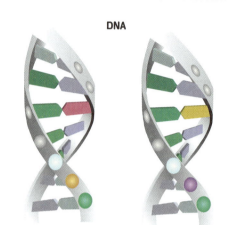

DNA

Animal Cells

Human cells, most animal cells and plant cells have the following parts:

- **Cytoplasm** – where most chemical reactions take place, including anaerobic respiration, the production of enzymes and other proteins.
- **Mitochondria** – contain the enzymes needed for aerobic respiration.
- A **nucleus** – contains the DNA that carries the genetic code for making enzymes and other proteins used in all chemical reactions in the cell.
- A **cell membrane** – allows chemicals like gases and water to pass in and out freely, but prevents other chemicals from leaving or entering the cell.

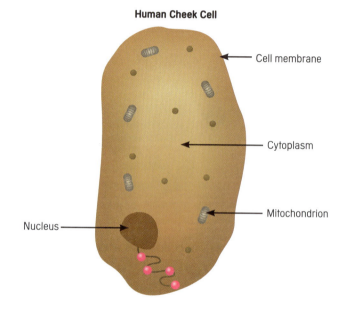

Human Cheek Cell

Cell membrane

Cytoplasm

Mitochondrion

Nucleus

Plant Cells

Plant cells also have the following parts:

- A **cell wall** – made of cellulose to strengthen the cell.
- A **permanent vacuole** – helps support the cell.
- **Chloroplasts** – contain the green pigment, chlorophyll (which absorbs light energy), and some enzymes needed for photosynthesis.

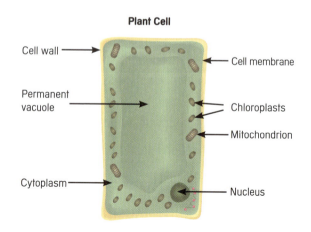

Plant Cell

Cell wall

Permanent vacuole

Cytoplasm

Cell membrane

Chloroplasts

Mitochondrion

Nucleus

DNA • Organelles • Nucleus

Microbial Cells

Most microbial cells, e.g. bacteria, have the following features:

- **Cell wall** – **not** made of cellulose but of other material, e.g. protein.

- **DNA** – in a circular structure **not** in a nucleus and **not** as chromosomes.

Yeast cells are more similar to higher organisms, but are still referred to as microbial cells.

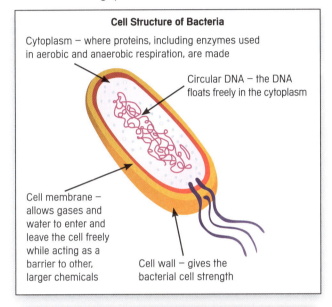

Cell Structure of Bacteria

Cytoplasm – where proteins, including enzymes used in aerobic and anaerobic respiration, are made

Circular DNA – the DNA floats freely in the cytoplasm

Cell membrane – allows gases and water to enter and leave the cell freely while acting as a barrier to other, larger chemicals

Cell wall – gives the bacterial cell strength

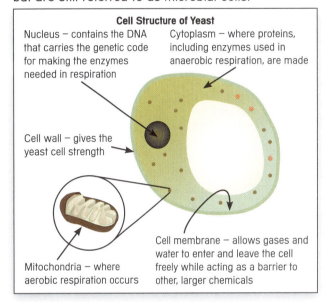

Cell Structure of Yeast

Nucleus – contains the DNA that carries the genetic code for making the enzymes needed in respiration

Cytoplasm – where proteins, including enzymes used in anaerobic respiration, are made

Cell wall – gives the yeast cell strength

Mitochondria – where aerobic respiration occurs

Cell membrane – allows gases and water to enter and leave the cell freely while acting as a barrier to other, larger chemicals

Enzymes

Enzymes are protein molecules that speed up the rate of chemical reactions in cells (i.e. they're catalysts in living things). Cells produce enzymes according to the instructions carried in genes (DNA code).

Enzymes need a specific temperature to work at their **optimum**. Different enzymes have different optimum working temperatures. The graph shows the effect of **temperature** on enzyme activity:

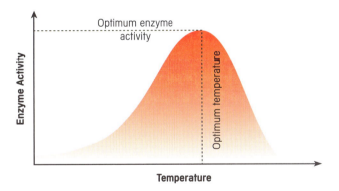

Optimum enzyme activity

Enzyme Activity

Optimum temperature

Temperature

- **HT** At low temperatures, small increases in temperature cause an increase in the frequency and energy of collisions between reactants and enzymes, so the rate of reaction increases.

- After the **optimum enzyme activity** is reached, the enzymes start to get damaged, so the reaction starts to slow down.

- Eventually the enzyme's structure is permanently destroyed and it stops working.

HT In other words, the enzyme has become **denatured**.

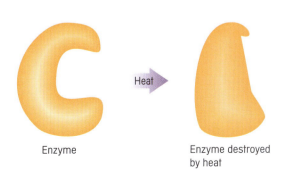

Enzyme

Heat

Enzyme destroyed by heat

B4 The Processes of Life

The Lock and Key Model

Only a molecule with the correct shape can fit into an enzyme. This is a bit like a **key** (the molecule) fitting into a **lock** (the enzyme). Once the enzyme and molecule are linked, the following happens:

1 The reaction takes place.

2 The products are released.

3 The process is able to start again.

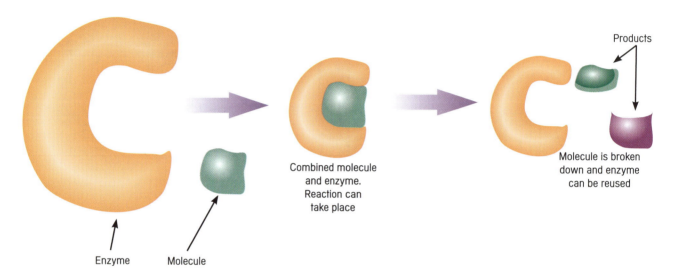

Enzyme   Molecule

Combined molecule and enzyme. Reaction can take place

Products

Molecule is broken down and enzyme can be reused

HT The Active Site

The **active site** is the place where the molecule fits into the enzyme. Each enzyme has a different **shape**, so it's highly specific.

The shape of the active site can be changed irreversibly by…

- **heating** the enzyme above a certain temperature
- altering the **pH level**.

This means the molecule can no longer fit and the reaction can't take place.

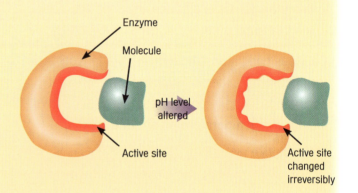

Enzyme

Molecule

Active site

pH level altered

Active site changed irreversibly

Respiration

Respiration is the **release of energy** from food chemicals in all living cells. There are two types of respiration:

- Aerobic respiration
- Anaerobic respiration.

Key Words   **Active site**

Aerobic Respiration

Aerobic respiration releases energy inside living cells by breaking down glucose and combining the products with **oxygen**.

Glucose **+** Oxygen ⟶ Carbon dioxide **+** Water **+** Energy released

HT The **symbol** equation for this is:

$$C_6H_{12}O_6 + 6O_2 \longrightarrow 6CO_2 + 6H_2O + \text{Energy released}$$

Aerobic respiration needs oxygen and occurs in animal cells, plant cells and in many microbial cells. The energy released is used in many chemical reactions, including…

- movement, e.g. the contraction of muscles when running
- the synthesis (making) of large molecules from smaller ones, e.g. chlorophyll from glucose

HT • **active transport** of some chemical molecules across a cell membrane.

Anaerobic Respiration

Anaerobic respiration releases energy inside the cytoplasm of living cells by breaking down glucose molecules **without the use of oxygen**.

In plant cells and in some microbial cells, e.g. yeast:

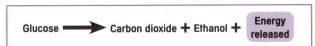

Glucose ⟶ Carbon dioxide **+** Ethanol **+** Energy released

In animal cells and in some bacteria:

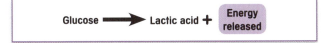

Glucose ⟶ Lactic acid **+** Energy released

Anaerobic respiration occurs in conditions of very low oxygen or where no oxygen is present. For example…

- when plant root cells are in waterlogged soil, e.g. rice plants
- in human muscle cells during vigorous exercise, e.g. a 100m sprint
- in bacterial cells inside a puncture wound.

Aerobic respiration is much more efficient and releases much more energy per glucose molecule (19 times more) than anaerobic respiration.

Quick Test

1. What is the function of mitochondria in a cell?
2. What are the three structures found in plant cells but not in animal cells?
3. What are enzymes?
4. What is respiration?
5. How is anaerobic respiration different from aerobic respiration?
6. **HT** What word describes an enzyme's structure when it's destroyed?

Uses of Anaerobic Respiration

Anaerobic respiration can be useful:

- It provides a little more energy to cells when very necessary, e.g. to limb muscles when running away from danger.
- In sewage farms, anaerobic microbes can be added to the solid matter. These microbes break down the sewage and release methane gas, which is collected. This gas, now called **biogas**, is burned to heat water to turn a generator for electricity. Alternatively, biogas can be used as a fuel to replace petrol in vehicles.

- Anaerobic respiration in yeast is used in baking. Yeast in bread dough releases carbon dioxide gas, which makes the dough rise before baking.
- Anaerobic respiration in yeast is also used in brewing to produce alcohol (ethanol) in wines and beers. This process is known as **fermentation**. If oxygen gets in, the yeast stops respiring anaerobically and the alcohol turns to vinegar (ethanoic acid), which ruins the product.

Synthesis of Large Molecules

Glucose, produced in photosynthesis in plants, can be built up into a **polymer** as cellulose (for building cell walls) or as starch (for storage in roots).
A polymer is a long-chain molecule made from copies of the same unit – in this case, glucose.

Glucose		Starch
Individual sugar molecules	→	Long chains of identical sugar molecules

Glucose and nitrates can be joined to make larger molecules of amino acids. In turn, amino acids can be joined together to make proteins (**polymers** of amino acids) in plant, animal and bacterial cells.

Forming a Protein Molecule

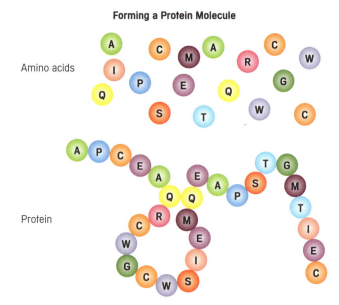

Amino acids

Protein

Photosynthesis

Photosynthesis takes place in three stages:

1. **Light energy** is absorbed by **chlorophyll** in green plants.
2. Within the chlorophyll molecule, the light energy is used to **rearrange** the **atoms** of carbon dioxide and water to produce glucose (a sugar).
3. Oxygen is produced as a **waste product**.

The equation for photosynthesis is:

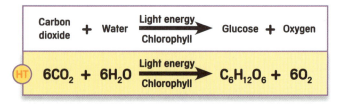

Carbon dioxide + Water $\xrightarrow[\text{Chlorophyll}]{\text{Light energy}}$ Glucose + Oxygen

HT $6CO_2 + 6H_2O \xrightarrow[\text{Chlorophyll}]{\text{Light energy}} C_6H_{12}O_6 + 6O_2$

Limiting Factors for Photosynthesis

Any one of the following factors can limit the rate of photosynthesis at a particular time:

- Temperature
- Carbon dioxide concentration
- Light intensity

Accurate measurements of the rate of photosynthesis can be hard because it's difficult to measure without altering one of the limiting factors. Factors that affect photosynthesis are difficult to control, e.g. wind or moisture levels.

Measurements only **indicate** the rate of photosynthesis rather than give a definite rate.

Temperature

1. As the temperature rises, so does the rate of photosynthesis. So, temperature is limiting the rate of photosynthesis.
2. As the temperature approaches 45°C, the enzymes controlling photosynthesis start to be destroyed and the rate of photosynthesis drops to zero.

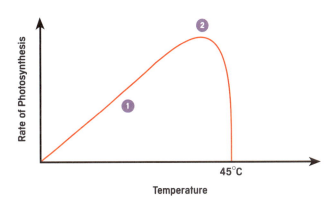

Carbon Dioxide Concentration

1. As the carbon dioxide concentration rises, so does the rate of photosynthesis. So, carbon dioxide is limiting the rate of photosynthesis.
2. A rise in carbon dioxide levels now has no effect. Carbon dioxide is no longer the limiting factor. It must be either light or temperature.

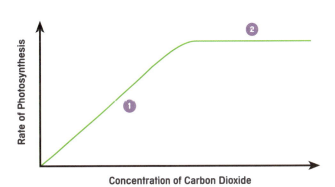

Light Intensity

1. As the light intensity increases, so does the rate of photosynthesis. So, light intensity is limiting the rate of photosynthesis.
2. A rise in light intensity now has no effect. Light intensity is no longer the limiting factor. It must be either carbon dioxide or temperature.

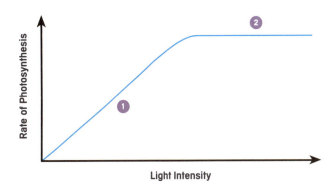

B4 The Processes of Life

Collecting Data about how Light Affects Plants

Data can be collected in the field to investigate how light affects plants:

- Light levels can be measured using a **light meter**.
- Plants can be identified using an **identification key**.
- Plants are chosen at random by using a **quadrat** and **transect**.

A **quadrat** is anything with a defined area, e.g. a half metre square, which is placed at intervals along the transect line randomly to sample the area.

A **transect** is a random section across an area, e.g. a line or measured band, which is used to represent the entire area.

In the transect shown opposite, the quadrats are placed at 20-metre intervals, which would provide a good sample of the changes occurring along the transect line from the forest to the beach.

These techniques are used to ensure that the data produced is **representative** of the area but is also **random** to avoid any **bias** in the findings.

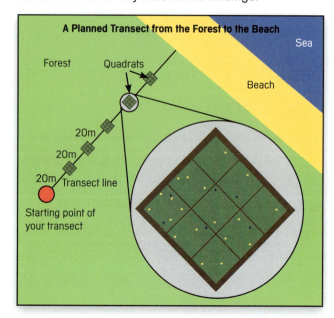

A Planned Transect from the Forest to the Beach

Diffusion

Diffusion is the overall movement of **substances** from regions of **high** concentration, to regions of **low** concentration.

Oxygen and carbon dioxide are exchanged in the **leaf** by diffusion of the gases in and out.

Substances that move in and out of **cells** by diffusion include oxygen, carbon dioxide and dissolved food.

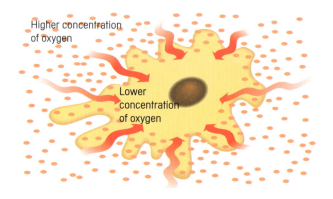

HT Energy Use in Plants

Plants need to absorb nitrates from the soil for healthy growth.

They normally absorb nutrients by **diffusion**, but the concentration of nitrates outside the plant is lower than that inside. Therefore, a plant has to use **energy** from respiration to absorb nitrates by **active transport**.

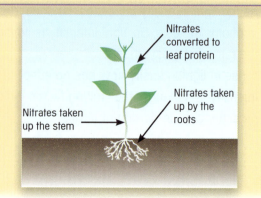

HT Active Transport

Some chemicals can also be moved by **active transport**. This is the movement of a substance against a concentration gradient (i.e. from a region of low concentration to a region of high concentration). It requires **energy** from respiration to do this.

For example, if the concentration of glucose inside a cell is higher than the concentration outside the cell, the glucose would diffuse out of the cell along the concentration gradient. So, cells use active transport to bring all of the glucose back inside the cell.

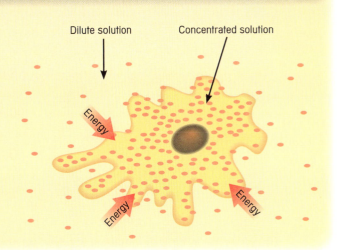

Dilute solution   Concentrated solution

Energy   Energy   Energy

Osmosis

Osmosis is a type of diffusion. It's the overall movement of **water** from a **dilute solution** to a more **concentrated solution** through a partially permeable membrane.

The membrane allows the passage of water molecules but not solute molecules, which are too large.

The water moving due to osmosis gradually **dilutes** the concentrated solution.

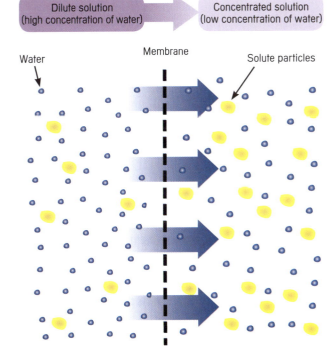

Dilute solution (high concentration of water)   Concentrated solution (low concentration of water)

Water   Membrane   Solute particles

Quick Test

1. What is the green pigment that absorbs light energy in a plant cell?
2. What is the waste product of photosynthesis?
3. What do plants need from the soil to add to glucose to make amino acids?
4. What is a transect?
5. What is diffusion?
6. What is the only substance moved by osmosis?

1 **(a)** The diagram shows a human cheek cell.

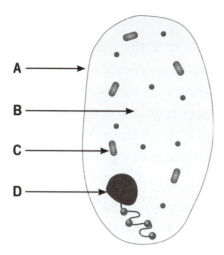

    (i) Write the letter that identifies the part where aerobic respiration takes place. .... **[1]**

    (ii) Write the letter that identifies the part which contains DNA. .... **[1]**

  (b) What is the function of mitochondria? **[1]**

2 Cherry did an experiment to investigate the effect of light intensity on the rate of photosynthesis in a pondweed. In order to do this, she placed a light at different distances from the pondweed and collected the gas given off in a 10-minute period. Her results are shown on the right:

Distance from Light (cm)	Volume of Gas (cm³)
10	24
20	15
30	8
40	4

  (a) What conclusion can Cherry make from these results? **[1]**

  (b) What is the name of the gas given off by the pondweed? **[1]**

  (c) Light intensity is a **limiting factor** on photosynthesis in this case. Name **one** other limiting factor on photosynthesis. **[1]**

3 Which of the following is the **incorrect** statement about aerobic respiration? Put a tick (✓) in the box next to the appropriate answer. **[1]**

Oxygen is used to break up glucose molecules. ☐

Ethanol is produced as a waste product. ☐

Energy is released and used in muscle contraction. ☐

Energy is released and used to build polymers in a cell. ☐

4 Hannah had two identical cylinders cut from the same potato. She placed one cylinder in a dish, labelled A, containing distilled water. She placed the other cylinder in a dish, labelled B, containing a strong sugar solution.

After 10 minutes she removed the potato cylinders. The cylinder from dish A had become very hard and stiff. The cylinder from dish B had become very soft and floppy.

(a) Why was it important to have the cylinders cut from the same potato? **[1]**

....

(b) What had caused the potato from dish A to go hard and stiff? **[1]**

....

(c) What had caused the potato from dish B to go soft and floppy? **[1]**

....

5 (a) Name **three** substances that are moved in and out of cells by diffusion. **[3]**

....

....

(b) Use the words provided to complete the following sentence about water movement into a cell. **[2]**

concentrated   partially   selectively   osmosis   diffusion   dilute   salt

When water moves across a .... permeable membrane from a

.... solution to a .... solution, it's called movement by

....

HT **6** This question is about enzymes.

(a) Some friends have just come out of a lesson about enzymes and are discussing it.

Sebastian
Enzymes are proteins.

Sarah
Enzymes work best at high temperatures.

Nicholas
Cells make enzymes according to instructions carried in the genes.

Adele
Enzymes are only involved in the breakdown of food in the gut.

Which two students give correct statements? **[2]**

.... and ....

(b) What is meant by the term **denatured**? **[1]**

....

B5 Growth and Development

The Development of Organisms

Living organisms are made up of cells. In multicellular organisms such as humans and plants…

- similar cells form a **tissue**
- groups of tissues form an **organ**
- groups of organs make up **systems** within the whole **organism**.

Cells divide by two processes:

- **Mitosis**
- **Meiosis**.

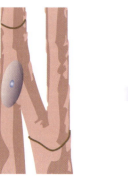

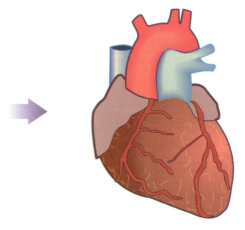

Cardiac muscle cell   Cardiac muscle tissue   Heart (organ)

Mitosis

Mitosis is the division of body cells to produce new cells. Each new cell has…

- **identical** sets of **chromosomes** as the parent cell
- the **same number** of chromosomes as the parent cell
- the same genes as the parent cell.

Mitosis occurs…

- for growth
- for repair
- to replace old tissues.

To enable mitosis to take place, cells go through a cycle of **growth** and then **division**. The cycle repeats itself until the cell can no longer divide.

When a cell enters the **growth phase** of the cycle…

- the number of **organelles increase**
- the **chromosomes** are **copied** – the two strands of each DNA molecule separate and new strands form alongside them.

When a cell enters the **division phase** of the cycle…

- the copies of the **chromosomes separate**
- the cell **divides**.

Parent cell with two pairs of chromosomes.   Each chromosome copies itself.   The copies are pulled apart. Cell now divides for the only time in this mitosis sequence.   Two 'daughter' cells are formed.

Key Words   **Tissue • Organ • Mitosis • Meiosis • Chromosome**

Growth and Development B5

Meiosis

Meiosis only takes place in the **testes** and **ovaries** and is a special type of cell division that produces **gametes** (sex cells, e.g. egg and sperm) for sexual reproduction.

Gametes contain **half** the number of chromosomes as the parent cell.

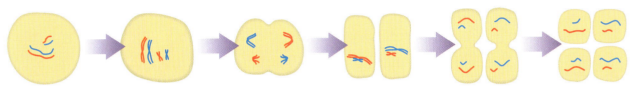

Cell with two pairs of chromosomes.

Each chromosome replicates itself.

Chromosomes part company and move to opposite sides with their 'copies'.

Cell divides for the first time.

Copies now separate and the second cell division takes place.

Four gametes, each with half the number of chromosomes as the parent cell.

Fertilisation

During **fertilisation** a **male gamete** (sperm) and a **female gamete** (egg) fuse together to produce a single body cell, called a **zygote**.

Gametes only have half the number of **chromosomes** as the parent cell, so the zygote that's produced has **one whole set** of chromosomes.

In each new pair of chromosomes...
- one chromosome comes from the father
- one chromosome comes from the mother.

The zygote then divides by **mitosis** to produce a cluster of cells called an **embryo**.

The embryo continues to divide by mitosis (from one cell to two, to four, to eight, etc.), after which the cells become specialised, until birth as a fully developed baby.

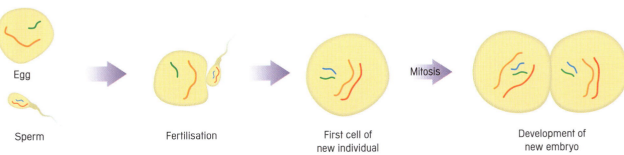

Egg

Sperm

Fertilisation

First cell of new individual – a zygote

Mitosis

Development of new embryo

B5 Growth and Development

Variation

Meiosis and **sexual reproduction** produce **variation** between offspring and parents:

- When the gametes fuse, genetic information from two individuals is combined.
- For each gene, just one of each parent's alleles is passed on.
- Each offspring can have a different combination of alleles from either parent.
- The offspring have different characteristics from each other.

Genes

Genes are present in the **chromosomes** in each cell **nucleus**.

Genes control…
- growth and development in organisms
- the development of characteristics, e.g. eye colour.

Genetic Code

Genes control **characteristics** by providing instructions for the production of **proteins**.

The instructions are in the form of a **code**, made up of **four bases** that hold the two strands of the double helix of the **DNA molecule** together. These bases always pair up in the same way:
- Adenine (A) pairs with thymine (T).
- Cytosine (C) pairs with guanine (G).

A gene is a small section of DNA within the chromosome. The order of the bases in the DNA section is the genetic code for the production of a particular protein. This is how the code determines the end characteristics of any organism.

A Section of DNA

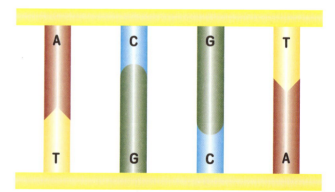

Controlling Growth and Development

DNA is **too large** to leave the nucleus. The genes therefore stay inside the nucleus but the production of proteins takes place **outside** the nucleus, in the **cytoplasm**.

Information stored in the genes has to be transferred into the cytoplasm.

This transfer is done in the following way:

1 The relevant section of DNA is unzipped.
2 Instructions are copied onto smaller molecules.

HT The smaller molecules are called **messenger RNA (mRNA)**.

3 These molecules leave the nucleus and carry the instructions to the **ribosomes**.
4 The ribosomes follow the instructions to make the relevant protein.

HT The sequence of bases in a gene determines the order in which **amino acids** are joined together to make a particular **protein**.

A group of **three** base pairs codes for one amino acid in a protein chain, called a **triplet code**. There are 20 different amino acids that can be made.

The structure of the protein depends on the amino acids that make it up.

This process is as follows:

1 DNA unravels at the correct gene.
2 A copy of the coding strand is made to produce mRNA.
3 The mRNA copy moves from the nucleus into the cytoplasm.
4 The triplet code is decoded by the ribosomes.
5 Amino acids are joined together to form a polypeptide (protein).

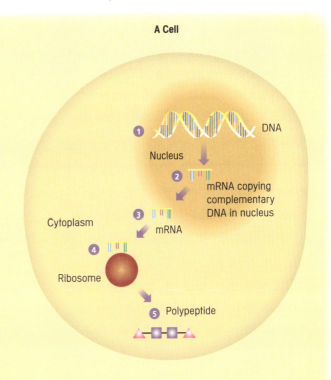

A Cell

1 DNA
Nucleus
2 mRNA copying complementary DNA in nucleus
3 mRNA
Cytoplasm
4
Ribosome
5 Polypeptide

Quick Test

1 What is a tissue?
2 Name the process by which body cells divide to produce new identical cells.
3 Where are gametes produced in the human body?
4 What is the name of the single cell produced after the fertilisation of an egg cell by a sperm cell?
5 What is the missing word? Adenine, cytosine, thymine and guanine are the four .... in a DNA molecule.
6 HT What carries the genetic information from the DNA in the nucleus to the cytoplasm?

B5 Growth and Development

Development of New Organisms

Up to the 8 cell stage, all cells in a human **embryo**…
- are unspecialised
- can have any gene switched on to form **any** kind of specialised cell.

These cells are known as **embryonic stem cells**.

After the 8 cell stage, the cells in an embryo…
- become **specialised**
- form different types of **tissue**.

The cells contain the **same genes**, but many genes are **not active** (switched off) because the cell only produces the **proteins** it needs to carry out its role. In specialised cells, only the genes needed for the cell to function are active (switched on) as it only requires specific proteins (mainly enzymes).

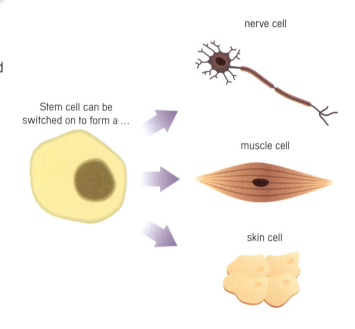

nerve cell

Stem cell can be switched on to form a …

muscle cell

skin cell

Stem Cells

Stem cells could potentially be used to…
- help treat diseases and disorders
- repair damage to various tissues.

There are three sources of stem cells:
1. Embryos
2. Blood from the umbilical cord
3. Adult stem cells from bone marrow.

Only the **embryonic stem cells** are completely unspecialised and can be used to form any cell type.

Ethical decisions need to be taken when using embryonic stem cells and this work is subject to government regulation.

HT In **therapeutic cloning**…
- the nucleus is removed from an egg cell and replaced with a nucleus from one of the patient's cells
- the egg cell is then stimulated so that it starts to divide (as if it were a zygote)
- at the 8 cell stage, cells can be removed as they're still unspecialised.

Adult stem cells will only produce cells of a certain type. For example, cells for creating blood cells in bone marrow have to be encouraged to grow more of that type of cell by reactivating (switching back on) inactive genes in the nuclei.

The advantage of using adult cells for growing replacement tissue is that they can be taken from the patient, so the patient's immune system will not reject the transplant.

Replacement tissue can be grown in a laboratory. Sometimes a 'host animal' (e.g. a mouse) is used to maintain a blood supply during growth.

Human ear

Host animal

Embryo • Stem cell • Therapeutic cloning

Differentiation in Plants

Plant cells divide by the process of **mitosis**.

New cells in plants specialise into the cells of…
* roots
* leaves
* flowers.

Unlike animals, most plants continue to grow in **height** and **width** throughout their lives.

Flowers

Leaves

Root

Meristems

Plant growth only occurs in areas called **meristems**, which are sites where **unspecialised cells** are dividing by **mitosis**.

These cells then…
* differentiate
* become specialised.

There are **two types** of meristem:
* **Lateral**, which leads to increased girth.
* **Apical**, which leads to increased height and longer roots.

Some plant cells remain **unspecialised** and can develop into any type of plant cell. These cells allow **clones** of plants with desirable features to be produced from **cuttings**.

If the **hormonal conditions** in their environment are changed, the unspecialised plant cells can develop into other…
* **tissues**, e.g. xylem and phloem
* **organs**, e.g. leaves, roots and flowers.

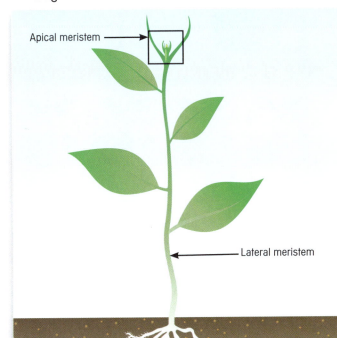

Apical meristem

Lateral meristem

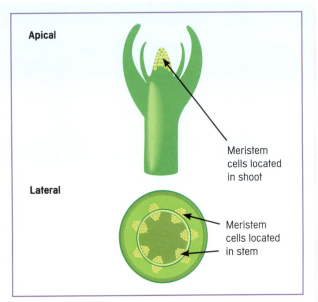

Apical

Lateral

Meristem cells located in shoot

Meristem cells located in stem

B5 Growth and Development

Xylem and Phloem

Xylem tubes are used by the plant to…

- transport water and soluble mineral salts from the roots to the stem and leaves
- replace water lost during transpiration and photosynthesis.

Phloem tubes are used by the plant to transport dissolved food to the whole plant for respiration or storage.

Cross-section of a Stem

Phloem vessels carry food substances up and down the plant

Xylem

Phloem

Xylem vessels carry water up from the roots

Cuttings

Plants can be reproduced in the following way:

1. Cuttings are taken from a plant.
2. The cuttings are put in a rooting hormone.
3. Roots start to form and the new plants develop.

The new plants are **genetically identical** to the parent plant, i.e. they are **clones**.

HT **Auxins** are the main plant hormones used in horticulture, which…

- affect cell division at the tip of a shoot
- cause cells to grow in size just under the tip so that the stem or roots grow longer.

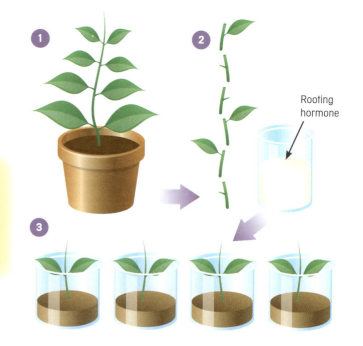

Rooting hormone

Phototropism

Plants respond to light by changing the direction in which they grow. This is called **phototropism**.

They grow towards a light source as they need light to survive.

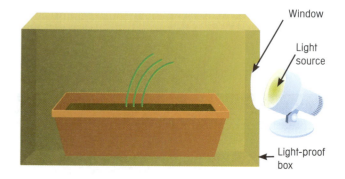

Window

Light source

Light-proof box

Clone • Auxin • Phototropism

HT How Phototropism Works

Auxin is produced at the shoot tip. It moves down the shoot, causing cells further down the shoot to grow.

When light shines on a shoot, auxin near the light source is slowly destroyed, so there's more auxin on the far side away from the light. This causes these cells to lengthen faster than those near the light, so the shoot bends towards the light. Experiments, like the ones below, have allowed scientists to achieve this explanation of phototropism.

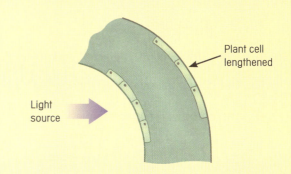

Plant cell lengthened

Light source

1 When a light source is directly overhead…
- auxin is evenly spread through the shoot
- the shoot grows **straight** up.

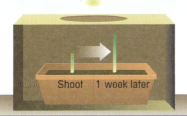

Shoot 1 week later

2 When a light source is at an angle…
- auxin is destroyed nearest to the light source
- the auxin is concentrated on the side furthest away from the light
- the shoot **bends** towards the light.

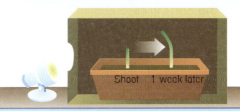

Shoot 1 week later

3 If the tip of the shoot is removed or covered in opaque material, then the plant will continue to grow upwards – as if the light source isn't there.

Opaque cap

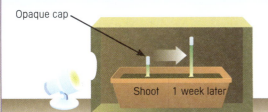

Shoot 1 week later

4 If the tip is covered with a transparent cap, then it will still grow towards the light source. The same thing will happen if an opaque cylinder is wrapped around the stem, leaving the tip exposed.

Transparent cap   Opaque cylinder

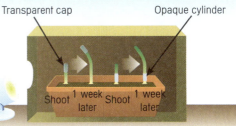

Shoot 1 week later Shoot 1 week later

Quick Test

1. What is the name given to the areas of plants where growth occurs?
2. Which tubes carry water up a plant?
3. Which tubes carry dissolved food in a plant?
4. What is needed for a cutting from a plant to develop roots?
5. Plants grow towards light. What is this called?

1 **(a)** These steps describe cell growth and division in the cell cycle. They're in the wrong order. Put the steps in the correct order by writing letters in the empty boxes. One has been done for you. **[2]**

    A The cell divides.

    B The number of organelles increases.

    C The chromosome copies move apart from one another.

    D The chromosomes are copied.

                         B | | |

(b) Name the **two** locations that the process of meiosis can take place in. **[2]**

(c) What is the name given to a fertilised cell? **[1]**

2 Jonah planted a seedling (a young plant) into a flowerpot and placed it in a greenhouse. His sister moved it so that the Sun only shone on it from one side.

Explain how the seedling would grow and why this would help it to survive. **[6]**

✐ *The quality of written communication will be assessed in your answer to this question.*

3 **(a)** What are the characteristics of stem cells? **[1]**

(b) Why can't stem cells be taken after the 8 cell stage? **[1]**

(c) Why are embryonic stem cells sometimes better to use than adult stem cells? **[1]**

4 Jonty was investigating the growth rate of different bacteria over a three-hour period. He began with a single bacterium and his table of results is below.

Type	30 minutes	60 minutes	90 minutes	120 minutes	150 minutes	180 minutes
A	2	8	12	16	32	64
B	4	16	64	256	1024	4096
C	2	8	16	16	32	64
D	4	16	32	128	256	1024

(a) Describe **two** differences between the pattern of results shown by type B and type D bacteria over the period of investigation. **[2]**

....

....

(b) Jonty concluded that the highest rate of cell division was between 30 and 60 minutes. Suggest one source of evidence in the table that doesn't support his conclusion. **[1]**

....

....

HT 5 **(a)** After a revision lesson about genes and DNA, five pupils discuss some of the main points.

Mark
The human DNA molecule is a circular shape.

Chloe
I think the DNA molecule has a double helix structure.

Imran
DNA is made of four bases which always pair up A with C and G with T.

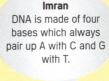
Emily
DNA is made of four bases which always pair up A with T and G with C.

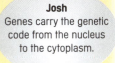
Josh
Genes carry the genetic code from the nucleus to the cytoplasm.

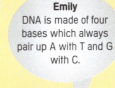

Which two pupils are giving correct statements? **[2]**

.... and ....

(b) DNA is too large to leave the cell. How does the genetic information leave the cell? **[1]**

....

B6 Brain and Mind

The Central Nervous System

A **stimulus** is a change in an organism's environment. Animals respond to **stimuli** in order to keep themselves in suitable conditions for survival.

An animal's response is coordinated by the **central nervous system** (**CNS**). This part of the system is sometimes referred to as the **processing centre**. The CNS (brain and spinal cord) is connected to the body by the **peripheral nervous system** (**PNS**).

The peripheral nervous system consists of…

- **sensory neurons** that carry impulses from **receptors** to the CNS
- **motor neurons** that carry impulses from the CNS to **effectors**.

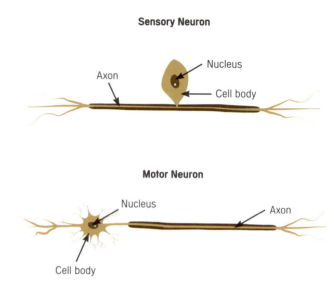

Sensory Neuron

Axon — Nucleus — Cell body

Motor Neuron

Nucleus — Axon — Cell body

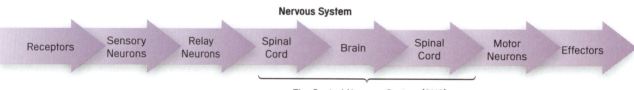

Nervous System

Receptors → Sensory Neurons → Relay Neurons → Spinal Cord → Brain → Spinal Cord → Motor Neurons → Effectors

The Central Nervous System (CNS)

Receptors and Effectors

Receptors and **effectors** can form part of complex organs, for example…

- muscle cells in a muscle
- light receptor cells in the retina of the eye
- hormone secreting cells in a gland.

Muscle cells in a muscle – impulses travel along motor neurons and stop at the muscle cells (effectors), causing the muscle cells to contract.

Light receptor cells in the retina of the eye – the lens focuses light onto receptor cells in the retina. The receptor cells are then stimulated and send impulses along sensory neurons to the brain.

Hormone secreting cells in a gland – an impulse travels along a motor neuron and stops at the hormone secreting cells in glands (effectors). This triggers the release of the hormone into the bloodstream.

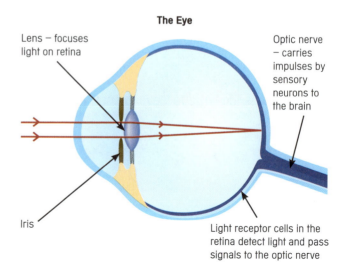

A Motor Neuron

Nucleus — Muscle fibre (effector) — Cell body

The Eye

Lens – focuses light on retina

Optic nerve – carries impulses by sensory neurons to the brain

Iris

Light receptor cells in the retina detect light and pass signals to the optic nerve

Stimulus • Central nervous system • Neuron • Receptor • Effector

Neurons

Neurons are specially-adapted cells that carry an **electrical signal** when stimulated:

- They are **elongated** (lengthened) to make connections between different parts of your body.
- They have **branched endings** so that a single neuron can act on many other neurons or effectors.

In **motor neurons** the cytoplasm forms a long fibre surrounded by a cell membrane called an **axon**.

Some axons are surrounded by a fatty sheath, which…

- insulates the neuron from neighbouring cells
- increases the speed at which the nerve impulse is transmitted.

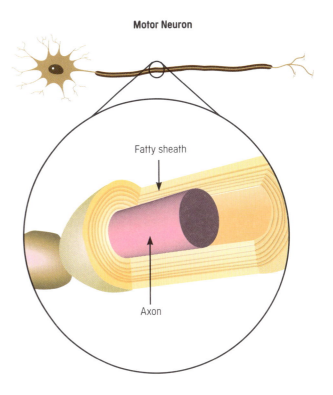

Motor Neuron

Fatty sheath

Axon

Synapses

Synapses are the gaps between adjacent neurons.

HT Impulses are transferred between neurons in the following way:

1. A nerve impulse reaches the synapse through the sensory neuron.
2. The impulse triggers the release of chemicals, called neurotransmitters, into the synapse.
3. Neurotransmitters diffuse across the synapse and bind with receptor molecules on the membrane of a motor neuron.
4. A nerve impulse is sent through the motor neuron.

The receptor molecules only bind with certain chemicals to start a nerve impulse in the motor neuron.

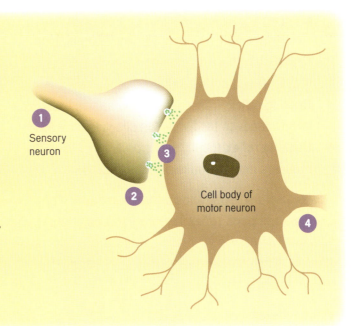

1 Sensory neuron

3

2

Cell body of motor neuron

4

B6 Brain and Mind

Reflex Actions

A **reflex action** is a fast, automatic, involuntary response to a **stimulus**.

The basic pathway for a reflex arc is as follows:
1. A **receptor** is stimulated (e.g. by a sharp pain).
2. This causes impulses to pass along a **sensory neuron** into the spinal cord.
3. The sensory neuron **synapses** with a relay neuron, by-passing the brain.
4. The relay neuron synapses with a motor neuron, sending impulses to the **effectors**.
5. The effectors **respond** (e.g. muscles contract).

Simple reflexes like these ensure that an animal **automatically responds** to a **stimulus** in a way that helps it to survive, for example…
- finding food
- sheltering from predators
- finding a mate.

> **HT** The fixed pathway of neurons in these actions allows the very rapid response as there isn't any processing of the information by the brain.

The majority of the behaviour displayed by simple animals is the result of **reflex actions**. The disadvantage of this is that the animals have difficulty responding to new situations.

Reflex Action Pathway

Stimulus → Receptor → Sensory Neuron → Relay Neuron (in spinal cord) → Motor Neuron → Effector → Response

Simple Reflexes in Humans

Newborn babies exhibit a range of simple reflexes:
- **Stepping reflex** – when held under its arms in an upright position, with feet on a firm surface, a baby makes walking movements with its legs.
- **Grasping reflex** – baby tightly grasps a finger that is placed in its hand.
- **Rooting reflex** – baby turns head and opens mouth ready to feed when its cheek is stroked.
- **Sucking reflex** – baby sucks on a finger (or mother's nipple) that is put in its mouth.

Adults also display a range of simple reflexes. For example, the **pupil reflex** in your eye stops bright light from damaging your retina. Your iris controls the amount of light that enters your eye by contracting various muscle fibres.

Other reflexes include…
- the 'knee-jerk' when the leg straightens if the knee joint is struck beneath the knee cap
- dropping a hot object when you grip it
- blinking when an object comes close to your face.

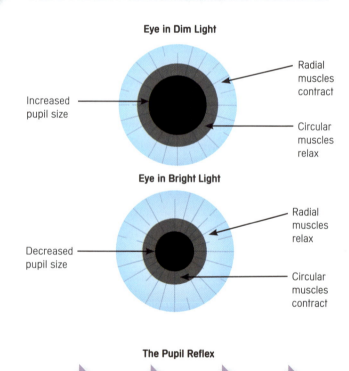

Eye in Dim Light

Increased pupil size

Radial muscles contract

Circular muscles relax

Eye in Bright Light

Decreased pupil size

Radial muscles relax

Circular muscles contract

The Pupil Reflex

Light on retina → Impulse via optic nerve to the brain → Impulse via motor nerve to iris muscles → Pupil changes size

Conditioned Reflexes

A reflex response to a new stimulus can be learned by building an association between the stimulus that naturally triggers the response (**primary stimulus**) and the new stimulus (**secondary stimulus**).

The resulting reflex is called a **conditioned reflex action**.

This effect was discovered at the beginning of the 20th century by a Russian scientist named Pavlov.

Pavlov carried out the following dog experiment:

1. A bell was rung repeatedly whenever meat was shown and given to the dog.
2. Eventually, ringing the bell without any meat present caused the dog to salivate.

A further example might be the feeling of hunger you get just by looking at the time on the clock. You've been conditioned to feel hungry at that time, even if you're not actually hungry.

HT In a conditioned reflex, the final response has **no direct connection** to the stimulus.

Some conditioned reflexes can increase a species' chance of survival.

For example, the caterpillar of the cinnabar moth is black and orange in colour, to warn predators that it's poisonous. After eating a few cinnabar caterpillars, a bird will start to associate these colours with a very unpleasant taste and avoid eating anything that is black and orange in colour.

In this way, a conditioned reflex may be regarded as simple learning.

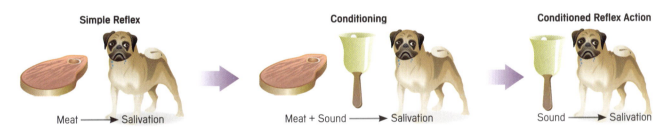

Simple Reflex — Meat ⟶ Salivation

Conditioning — Meat + Sound ⟶ Salivation

Conditioned Reflex Action — Sound ⟶ Salivation

HT Modifying Reflex Actions

In some situations your brain can override or modify a reflex action by sending a signal, via a neuron, to the motor neuron in the reflex arc.

For example, this modification allows you to keep hold of a hot plate even though your body's natural reflex response is to drop it.

Quick Test

1. What is a stimulus?
2. What type of neuron carries impulses from the central nervous system to an effector such as a muscle?
3. What is the name of a gap between two neurons?
4. What is the name of the long fibre attached to the cell body in a motor neuron?
5. What is a reflex action?
6. What is the name given to the type of action when the final response has no direct connection to the stimulus?

B6 Brain and Mind

Neuron Pathways

Mammals have **complex brains** that contain billions of **neurons**. This allows them to learn from experience, including how to respond to different situations (**social behaviour**).

In mammals **neuron pathways** are formed in the brain during development.

The brain grows rapidly during the first few years after birth. As each neuron matures, it sends out multiple branches, increasing the number of **synapses**.

The way in which a mammal interacts with its environment determines which pathways are formed:

1. Each time you have a new experience, a different neuron pathway is stimulated.
2. Every time the experience is repeated after that, the pathway is strengthened.
3. Pathways that aren't used regularly are eventually deleted.
4. Only the pathways that are activated most frequently are preserved.

These modifications mean that certain pathways of your brain become more likely to transmit impulses than others and you will learn how to do a task.

This is why you're able to learn some skills through **repetition**, for example, riding a bicycle, revising for an exam or playing a musical instrument.

A **PET** (Positron Emission Tomography) **scan** provides a 3D image, which shows neuron activity in parts of the brain in response to learning words through…

* hearing them
* seeing them
* speaking them.

The areas that are stimulated the most develop more synapses between neurons.

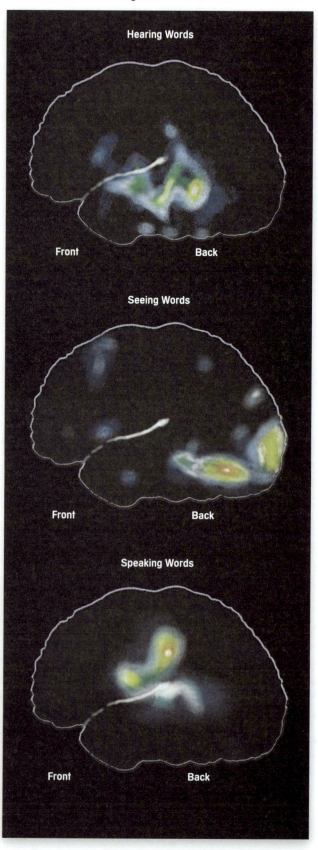

Image of a PET Scan

Hearing Words

Front | Back

Seeing Words

Front | Back

Speaking Words

Front | Back

Key Words   **Neuron • Synapse**

Children

Child Development

After children are born, there are a series of developmental milestones that can be checked to see if development is following normal patterns.

If the milestones are missing or late it could mean that…

- there are neurological problems
- the child is lacking stimulation.

For example…

- at three months, babies should be able to lift their heads when held to someone's shoulder
- at 12 months, babies should be able to hold a cup and drink from it.

Feral Children

Evidence suggests that children only learn some skills at particular stages in their development.

One example of evidence showing this comes from the study of language development in 'feral children'.

Feral children have been isolated from society in some way, so they don't go through the normal development process.

This isolation can be deliberate (e.g. keeping a child alone in a locked room) or accidental (e.g. through being shipwrecked).

In the absence of any other humans, the children don't ever gain the ability to talk, other than to make rudimentary grunting noises.

Learning a language later in development is a much harder and slower process.

Adapting

The variety of potential pathways in the brain makes it possible for animals to **adapt** to new situations.

For example…

- dogs can be trained to follow spoken commands
- dolphins in captivity can be trained to collect food from a person's hand.

Coordination of Senses

The evolution of a large brain, containing billions of neurons, gave humans a better chance of survival due to the ability to arrive at complex conclusions quickly in different situations.

Intelligence, memory, language and consciousness (a sense of right and wrong) are some of the skills that enable human survival. These are all dealt with in the **cerebral cortex** area of the brain.

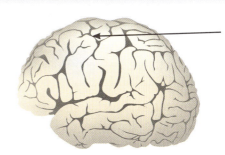

Cerebral cortex

Key Words | Cerebral cortex

B6 Brain and Mind

Mapping the Cortex

Scientists have used different methods to map the regions of the cerebral cortex:

- Physiological techniques
- Electronic techniques
- Magnetic Resonance Images (MRI) scanning.

Physiological techniques – damage to different parts of the brain can produce different problems, e.g. memory loss, paralysis or speech loss. Studying the effects of this has led to an understanding of which parts of the brain control different functions.

Electronic techniques – an electroencephalogram (EEG) is a visual record of the electrical activity generated by **neurons** in the brain. Electrodes are placed on the scalp to pick up the electrical signals. By stimulating the patient's **receptors**, the parts of the brain that respond can be mapped.

Magnetic Resonance Imaging (MRI) scanning
– this is a relatively new technique that can be used to produce images of different cross-sections of the brain. The computer-generated picture uses colour to represent different levels of electrical activity. The activity in the brain changes depending on what the person is doing or thinking.

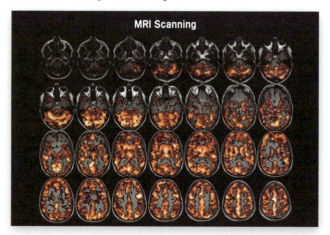

MRI Scanning

Memory

Memory is the ability to **store** and **retrieve** information. It can be divided into…

- **short-term memory** – stores information for a limited period of time
- **long-term memory** – stores an unlimited amount of information.

Many scientists have produced **models** to try to explain how the brain stores information, e.g. the **multi-store model**. This model states that short-term memory can be rehearsed so that it enters long-term storage.

Like many models though, this doesn't fully explain memory, as it's been found that information **doesn't** need short-term rehearsal to be stored as long-term memory. So, scientists may disagree about the explanations but continue their research to try to support or reject hypotheses to achieve a better conclusion.

Why we **forget** isn't fully explained by the model either. The reasons may be…

- **physical** – neurons decaying, e.g. in Alzheimer's disease
- **lack of retrieval** – if we don't use the information for a long time, the pathway is lost.

You're more likely to remember information if…
- it's repeated (especially over an extended period of time)
- there's a strong **stimulus** associated with it, e.g. colour, light, smell or sound
- you can see a pattern in it or impose a pattern on it, e.g. the order of the planets can be remembered by imposing a pattern: **M**r **V**enus's **e**lephant **m**akes **j**am **s**itting **u**pon **n**ectarines – **M**ercury, **V**enus, **E**arth, **M**ars, **J**upiter, **S**aturn, **U**ranus and **N**eptune.

Drugs and the Nervous System

Some drugs and toxins, e.g. Ecstasy, beta blockers and Prozac, affect the nervous system by changing the speed at which nerve impulses travel to the brain.

They can also…

- send false signals to the brain
- prevent nerve impulses from travelling across **synapses**
- overload the nervous system with too many nerve impulses.

HT **Serotonin** is a chemical transmitter used in the **central nervous system**. It can have mood-enhancing effects, i.e. it's associated with feeling happy.

Serotonin passes across the brain's synapses, landing on receptor molecules. Serotonin not on a receptor is absorbed back into the transmitting neuron by the transporter molecules.

Ecstasy (MDMA) blocks the transporter sites causing serotonin to build up in the synapse. This causes…

- serotonin concentrations in the brain to increase
- the user to experience feelings of elation.

The neurons are harmed in this process and memory loss can be caused in the long term.

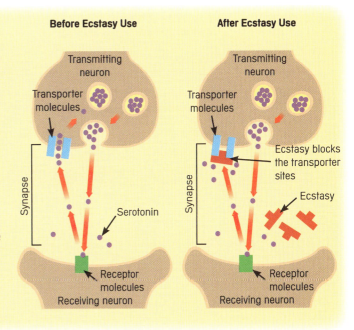

Coordination in the Body

All nervous responses can bring about fast responses, but they don't last long – they're immediate and short-lived.

Hormones produced in glands (e.g. insulin, adrenalin and oestrogen) travel in the blood and so can move all around the body. The response can last a lot longer in this way but is slower to act.

Both of these systems, nervous and chemical, are necessary to control the body's functions and have evolved in many multicellular organisms.

Quick Test

1. What develop in the human brain to allow learning from experience, e.g. language?
2. Which part of the brain is most concerned with intelligence and memory?
3. Name the technique that produces images of cross-sections of the brain.
4. What is memory?
5. What is the 'type' of memory when the brain only stores information for a limited time?
6. How do drugs like Ecstasy and Prozac affect the nervous system?

1 **(a)** Put a (ring) around the correct choice to complete each sentence.

    (i) Animals respond to stimuli. These responses are coordinated by the **central nervous system** / **peripheral nervous system**.   **[1]**

    (ii) The system making up the connections of sensory and motor neurons is called the **central nervous system** / **peripheral nervous system**.   **[1]**

(b) What type of neurons do the diagrams below show?

    (i)   **[1]**

    (ii)   **[1]**

(c) What does a motor neuron do to a hormone secreting gland when a message is sent?   **[1]**

(d) Give **two** functions of the fatty sheath surrounding the axon.   **[2]**

(e) What are synapses?   **[1]**

(f) How do drugs in general affect the nervous system?   **[1]**

2 Raul picks up a plate with his dinner on it and immediately drops it because it's far too hot. This is an example of a reflex action. Explain as fully as you can the sequence of events that take place in Raul's nervous system for this to happen.   **[6]**

    🖉 *The quality of written communication will be assessed in your answer to this question.*

3 The following table shows the reaction times of a patient who has been given varying doses of a drug.

Drug Dose	Time Taken to React (seconds)		
	Experiment 1	Experiment 2	Experiment 3
Nil	1.02	1.04	1.02
Small	1.32	1.08	1.04
Medium	1.18	1.19	1.24
Large	2.30	2.40	2.42

(a) Which of the reaction times appears to be an outlier? [1]

....

(b) What conclusion can you suggest from the data? [1]

....

(c) Why was each reaction time repeated three times? [1]

....

4 What is needed before biologists will accept a new theory on memory?
Put ticks (✓) in the boxes next to the **three** correct answers. [2]

The theory must…

…have a scientific mechanism. ☐   …be easy to understand. ☐

…be from a qualified biologist. ☐   …be published. ☐

…have data with high variability. ☐   …be repeatable. ☐

HT 5 (a) These steps describe the sequence of nerve impulse transmission. They're in the wrong order.
Put the steps into the correct order by writing the letters in the empty boxes. One has been done
for you. [3]

A Nerve impulse is sent through motor neuron.

B Chemical neurotransmitters are released into synapse.

C Neurotransmitters bind with receptors on motor neuron.

D Nerve impulse moves through sensory neuron.

E Neurotransmitters diffuse across.

D				

(b) Which drug blocks the sites in the brain's synapses where serotonin is removed? [1]

....

The Skeletal System

Vertebrates have an internal skeleton that…

- provides **support**
- enables **movement**
- **protects** internal organs.

Bones, muscles, tendons and ligaments combine so that joints can move easily and carry out work:

- **Bones** are rigid tissues that make up the skeleton.
- **Muscle** is tissue that contracts and relaxes.
- **Ligaments** are tough, fibrous, elastic connective tissues that connect **bones** together in a joint.
- **Tendons** are tough, fibrous, elastic connective tissues that connect **muscle to bone** or **muscle to muscle**.

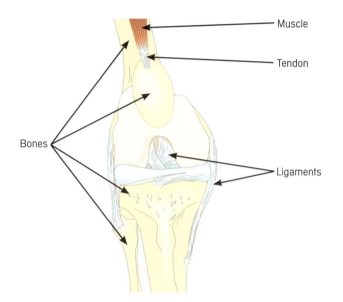

Joint Movement

Muscles can only move bones by **contracting** (getting shorter), so they work in antagonistic pairs, i.e. one muscle contracts while another muscle relaxes. For example…

- to lift the lower arm, the biceps contracts and the triceps relaxes
- to lower the arm, the triceps contracts and the biceps relaxes.

If the tendon connecting the triceps to the bone was cut, the triceps wouldn't be able to contract and the arm would remain in the up position.

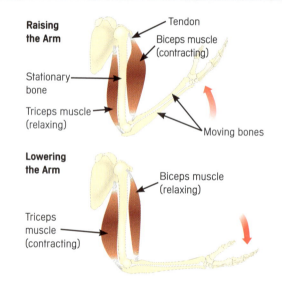

Synovial Joint

Joints are covered by a smooth layer of **cartilage**. Cartilage is a tough connective tissue that helps reduce wear and tear in a joint by preventing the bones rubbing together.

Synovial fluid is an oily fluid. It enables the joint to move freely by reducing friction and cushioning the joint against bumps and knocks.

Ligaments are tough and elastic to allow movement and, at the same time, hold the bones of the joint in position.

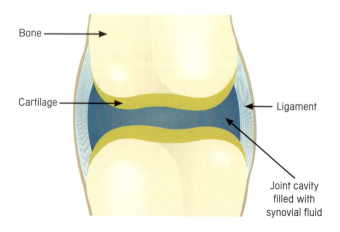

Medical History Assessment

Practitioners, for example, doctors, registered nurses, fitness instructors and opticians, are specially trained to help you maintain and improve your health and fitness.

Before they can recommend treatment or an exercise programme, a practitioner needs to know about a patient's medical or lifestyle history. Some of the key information they need to know is shown in the table below.

A practitioner must properly assess a patient before any diagnostic tests are carried out, in order to make sure that the treatment recommended is effective and will not make their condition worse, or cause another problem.

The risk of carrying out any tests must be assessed and balanced against the chances of being able to cure or reduce the **symptoms** (visible or noticeable effects on the body, which can be used to identify a problem).

Factors Considered	Details
Current medication	Different medicines can sometimes conflict with one another
Alcohol consumption	Excessive alcohol intake can cause… • weight gain • damage to the liver and kidneys • interference with some medications
Tobacco consumption	Smoking has been directly linked with… • lung cancer • heart disease • high blood pressure
Family medical history	Some medical conditions can be genetic (inherited). It's important to know if any particular conditions run in your family
Previous treatments	It you have recurring symptoms you might need a different **diagnosis** or to see a specialist

Treatment

Depending on the **diagnosis**, the practitioner will decide which treatment or method will be used to improve the patient's health or fitness.

There is often more than one way to achieve an agreed target. For example, the problem could be solved by…
- greater levels of fitness
- a period of recovery
- rehabilitation, e.g. learning how to walk again after an accident.

All treatments carry some risk. For example, a treatment could cause further harm or have side effects. The practitioner has to weigh the known risks against the benefits gained.

The patient must be made aware of the risks and likelihood of success, so that they can make an informed decision before consenting.

B7 Further Biology (Peak Performance)

Monitoring and Assessing Progress

A treatment or fitness training programme needs to be monitored to check that it's having the desired effect. It can then be modified depending on the patient's progress.

A programme might be modified before completion if…
- the patient is finding the programme too hard (the problem could continue or a new injury could occur)
- the patient is finding the programme too easy (progress would be slow and the patient might not recover fast enough).

One way of monitoring progress during training is to measure the **pulse rate** or **aerobic fitness** of a patient / client. A patient who is **increasing** their aerobic fitness should **lower** their heart rate and have a **faster recovery** rate. Resting blood pressure should also be **reduced** by a fitness programme.

The graph shows the effect of exercise on the heart rate and blood pressure.

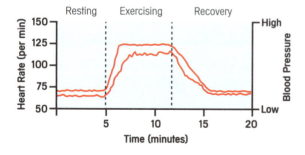

Regular contact between a patient and a practitioner has many benefits:

- The practitioner has the opportunity to become more familiar with the medical history and background of the patient.
- The patient will feel more comfortable and reassured if they see the same practitioner each time.

After treatment or training is complete, the patient can be called back for a check-up. Questions about progress and issues are asked and sometimes tests are carried out, e.g. the pulse rate might be checked.

A measurement of **body mass index (BMI)** can be used as a fitness indicator. BMI is worked out using the equation:

$$BMI = \frac{\text{Body mass (kg)}}{[\text{Height (m)}]^2}$$

The BMI number can be compared with a chart to provide a simple indicator of fitness level. BMI doesn't actually measure body-fat levels – to do this, you need to use a simple meter. An excess of body fat would be an indicator of poor fitness.

Practitioners may disagree about treatment or fitness programmes and their effects. This may be due to…
- their previous experiences with patients
- values such as BMI, for example, only being an **indicator** (i.e. not an absolute measure) of fitness levels.

Recording Progress

It's essential that accurate records are kept during treatment or fitness training because the records can be used to assess progress and determine trends.

HT Inaccurate records could slow down progress or even make a condition worse. However, progress records need to take into account the accuracy and repeatability of the recording techniques.

Injuries Caused by Excessive Exercise

If a person over-exerts themselves by doing excessive exercise, they can cause themselves the following injuries:

- **Sprains**
- **Dislocations**
- Torn **ligaments** or **tendons**.

Sprains

The following are **symptoms** of a sprain:

- **Swelling** due to fluid building up at the site of the sprain.
- **Pain** – the joint hurts and may throb.
- **Redness** and **warmth** caused by increased blood flow to the injured area.

Treatment for a sprain is in the form of RICE:

- **Rest** – the patient should rest and not move the injured part of the body.
- **Ice** – should be placed on the injury location for short periods (wrapped in suitable fabric to prevent ice burns) to reduce swelling and bleeding.
- **Compression** – gentle pressure should be applied with a bandage to reduce the build-up of the fluid that causes swelling.
- **Elevation** – the injured body part should be raised (to reduce blood pressure, which would then lead to less blood flow and swelling).

Physiotherapy

A **physiotherapist** specialises in the treatment of skeletal-muscular injuries. Physiotherapists help patients re-train or reuse a part of their body that isn't functioning properly. This is normally achieved with various exercises to strengthen muscles that have become weakened.

For example, the following exercise programme could be used to treat an injured leg:

- Warm up the joint by riding a stationary exercise bicycle, then straighten and raise the leg.

- Extend the leg while sitting (a weight may be worn on the ankle for this exercise).
- Raise the leg while lying on the stomach.
- Exercise in a pool, for example, walk as fast as possible in chest-deep water, perform small flutter kicks while holding onto the side of the pool, and raise each leg to 90° in chest-deep water while pressing the back against the side of the pool.

B7 Further Biology (Peak Performance)

Parts of Blood

The functions of the four components of blood are as follows:

- Red blood cells – these cells carry oxygen. They are packed with the red pigment, haemoglobin, which binds with oxygen. To make more room for the haemoglobin, red blood cells have no nucleus.

> **HT** Red blood cells have a biconcave shape which increases the surface area for more efficient uptake of oxygen.

- White blood cells – these cells fight infection and defend the body against microorganisms.
- Platelets – they clot together at injury sites to prevent blood loss.

- Plasma – a liquid that transports nutrients (e.g. glucose, mineral salts and amino acids), hormones, antibodies and waste (e.g. carbon dioxide and urea) around the body.

Platelets

Plasma

White blood cells

Red blood cells

The Heart

Most of the heart wall is made of muscle. The left side is more muscular than the right because it pumps blood around the whole body (whereas the right side pumps blood only to the lungs).

The heart has four chambers:

- Two **atria** – the smaller, less muscular upper chambers that receive blood coming back to the heart from the veins.
- Two **ventricles** – the larger, more muscular lower chambers that pump blood out of the heart.

The heart muscle needs a good blood supply of oxygen and glucose for respiration. This is supplied by the **coronary artery**, which is a branch from the aorta to the heart muscle.

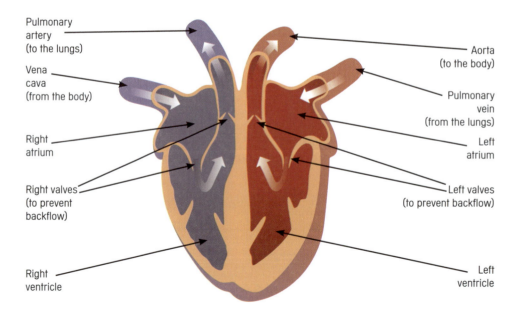

Pulmonary artery (to the lungs)

Vena cava (from the body)

Right atrium

Right valves (to prevent backflow)

Right ventricle

Aorta (to the body)

Pulmonary vein (from the lungs)

Left atrium

Left valves (to prevent backflow)

Left ventricle

The Double Circulatory System

This is the cardiac cycle:

- The heart muscles **relax** and blood flows into the atria through veins from the lungs and the rest of the body.
- The atria **contract**, squeezing blood into the ventricles.
- The ventricles **contract** and blood is forced out of the lower chambers, which carry the blood to the body and lungs.
- The heart muscles **relax** and the whole process starts again.

Valves in the heart and veins ensure that the blood flows in the right direction (i.e. not backwards).

Humans have a double circulation system, which means that the blood returns to the heart twice on every circuit of the body:

- Deoxygenated blood that has travelled around the body enters the heart via the right atrium.
- It's pumped from the heart into the lungs, where haemoglobin binds to the oxygen, becoming oxyhaemoglobin.
- The oxygenated blood returns to the heart via the left atrium and is then pumped to the rest of the body.

This system delivers glucose and oxygen to the muscles and carries waste products like carbon dioxide away from the muscles.

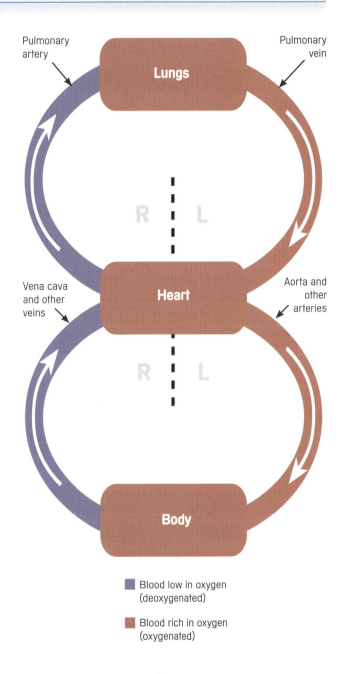

Pulmonary artery

Lungs

Pulmonary vein

R   L

Vena cava and other veins

Heart

Aorta and other arteries

R   L

Body

■ Blood low in oxygen (deoxygenated)

■ Blood rich in oxygen (oxygenated)

Quick Test

1. What are the tough, fibrous tissues that connect bone to muscle?
2. What are the pair of muscles that work opposite to each other called?
3. Give the formula for working out the body mass index (BMI).
4. Give three main symptoms of a sprain.
5. What is the function of red blood cells?
6. Name the main artery carrying blood from the heart to the rest of the body (not to the lungs).

Blood Vessels

There are three types of blood vessel:

- **Arteries** carry blood away from the heart towards the organs. They have thick, elastic walls to cope with the high pressure of blood coming from the heart. Substances can't pass through the artery walls.

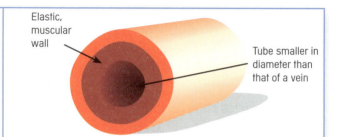

Elastic, muscular wall

Tube smaller in diameter than that of a vein

- **Veins** carry blood from the organs back to the heart. They have thinner, less elastic walls and contain valves to prevent the blood flowing backwards. Substances can't pass through the vein walls.

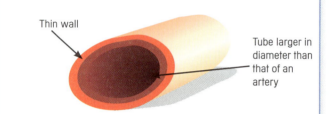

Thin wall

Tube larger in diameter than that of an artery

- **Capillaries** connect arteries to veins. They have a narrow, thin wall that is only one cell thick. The exchange of substances between cells and the blood takes place here.

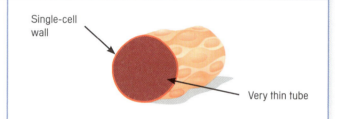

Single-cell wall

Very thin tube

HT Tissue Fluid

The plasma of arterial blood contains the dissolved products from digestion. Around the body tissues are networks of capillaries called **capillary beds**. The blood flow in capillary beds is very slow, so plasma leaves and becomes **tissue fluid**.

Tissue fluid…

- enables the nutrients required by the cells (e.g. glucose needed for respiration, oxygen and hormones) to diffuse into the tissue cells
- collects and carries away some cellular waste products, such as carbon dioxide and urea.

Most of the tissue fluid returns to the capillary bed where it again becomes plasma and continues its journey through the body, this time in the veins.

A Capillary Bed

Eventual return to blood through the lymphatic system

Lymph vessel

Lymphatic capillaries

Arterial capillaries

Vein

Venous capillaries

Tissue cells

Artery

Artery • Vein • Capillary

Body Temperature

Energy loss and **energy gain** from your body need to be balanced so that your body temperature remains **constant**.

The temperature of your body's extremities tends to be cooler than your core body temperature. Energy is transferred from the **blood** to the **tissues** when it reaches the cooler parts.

Controlling body temperature requires…

- **temperature receptors in the skin** to detect the external temperature
- **temperature receptors in the brain** to measure the temperature of the blood
- **the brain**, which acts as a processing centre to receive information from the temperature receptors and respond by triggering the **effectors**
- **effectors** (sweat glands and muscles) to carry out the automatic response.

If your body temperature is **too high**, heat needs to be transferred to the environment. This is done by **sweating**, since **evaporation** from the skin requires heat energy from the body.

If your body temperature is **too low**, your body will start to **shiver**. Shivering is the rapid **contraction** and release of muscles. These contractions require energy from increased **respiration**, and heat is released as a by-product, warming surrounding tissue.

Sweating   Shivering

HT Vasodilation and Vasoconstriction

Blood temperature is monitored by a centre in your brain called the **hypothalamus**.

In **hot conditions** blood vessels in the skin **dilate**, allowing more blood to flow through the skin capillaries. This means that more heat is lost from the surface of the skin by radiation. This is called **vasodilation**.

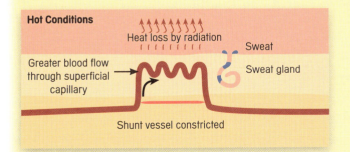

Hot Conditions
Heat loss by radiation
Sweat
Greater blood flow through superficial capillary
Sweat gland
Shunt vessel constricted

In **cold conditions** blood vessels in the skin **constrict**, reducing the amount of blood that flows through the skin capillaries.

This means that less heat is lost from the surface of the skin by radiation. This is called **vasoconstriction**.

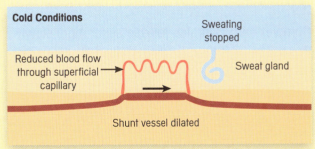

Cold Conditions
Sweating stopped
Reduced blood flow through superficial capillary
Sweat gland
Shunt vessel dilated

These responses are examples of effectors working **antagonistically** (opposite to each other) to restrict or increase blood flow near the skin surface. This allows a very sensitive and controlled response, in this case to allow a gradual increase or decrease in blood flow, depending on the strength of the stimulus. This means that the body temperature doesn't get too high or low.

Control of Blood Sugar Level

After a meal the digestion of carbohydrates leads to sugar being found in the blood. The pancreas deals with the rising blood sugar level by releasing a hormone called insulin. Insulin makes cells remove sugar from the blood. Cells use the sugar for functions such as respiration. If the hormone release goes wrong for any reason, it leads to diabetes.

There are two types of diabetes:
- **Type 1** – occurs when the pancreas stops producing enough insulin. This type is often genetic. It can be controlled by insulin injections and diet.
- **Type 2** – occurs when the body stops responding to its own insulin or doesn't make enough insulin. This type is often caused by old age, or as a result of a poor diet or obesity, and is sometimes referred to as **late-onset diabetes**. It can be controlled by diet and exercise.

The sugars like those found in processed foods are called **simple carbohydrates**. Other types of sugar, like those found in fruit, are called **complex carbohydrates**.

Simple carbohydrates release sugar quickly into the bloodstream, causing a rapid rise in blood sugar level.

Complex carbohydrates release sugar more slowly into the bloodstream, so they're more likely to help maintain a constant sugar level.

Soluble fibre, found in fruit, oats and beans, for example, can release sugar slowly from digestion in the intestine and this can help to prevent blood sugar levels becoming too high.

An unhealthy diet may not only cause diabetes but can also lead to obesity, heart disease and some cancers, e.g. of the bowel. Regular exercise can help to maintain a healthy body mass and fitness because it helps to use up sugar, rather than store it.

The graph shows the number of people aged under 16 whose obesity played a part in their admission to hospital over a 10-period year in a particular country. Obesity is linked to dietary patterns and so the graph highlights how lifestyle changes may affect health.

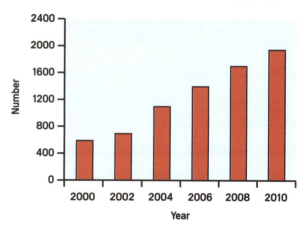

Obesity-related Hospital Admissions for Under 16s

Quick Test

1. How does shivering help to raise your body temperature?
2. Name the hormone that's released to cause sugar to be taken from the blood by cells.
3. What is the difference between type 1 and type 2 diabetes?
4. Why are complex carbohydrates more likely to maintain body sugar levels than simple carbohydrates?

Learning from Natural Ecosystems

In a perfect, stable ecosystem there is no waste because the output from one part of the system becomes the input to another part. The waste materials from one part of the ecosystem are used as food or reactants by another part. This type of system is known as a **closed loop system**.

In stable ecosystems any output (loss) must be balanced by input (gain).

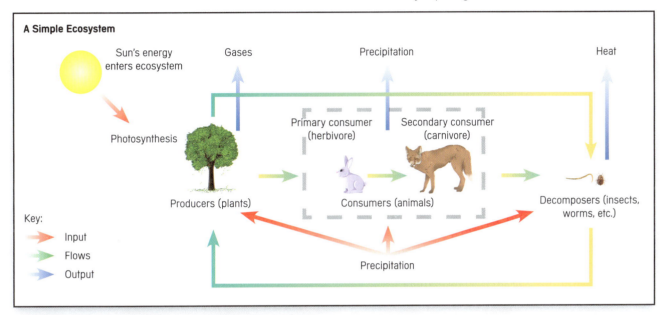

A Simple Ecosystem

Sun's energy enters ecosystem

Gases

Precipitation

Heat

Photosynthesis

Primary consumer (herbivore)

Secondary consumer (carnivore)

Producers (plants)

Consumers (animals)

Decomposers (insects, worms, etc.)

Precipitation

Key:
- Input
- Flows
- Output

Waste Products

In any natural ecosystem (e.g. a rainforest), the waste products include…

- **oxygen** from photosynthesis – this is used in respiration
- **carbon dioxide** from respiration – this is used in photosynthesis
- **dead matter** of living things (e.g. the remains of bodies, fallen leaves, petals, fruits, pollen, sperm, eggs and faeces) – this is used either directly as food or decomposed by microorganisms.

In order to survive, many organisms produce large quantities of reproductive structures (e.g. eggs, pollen and fruit) to ensure successful reproduction. However, this excess isn't wasted as it acts as input to other processes (e.g. the food chain).

As shown in the carbon and nitrogen cycles (see pages 27–28), microorganisms are extremely important in the recycling of waste:

- They digest and break down many different materials.
- They have many digestive enzymes that other organisms lack, e.g. for breaking down cellulose and wood, which couldn't be reused in the system otherwise.

However, in practice, no system is perfect. Even in our most stable systems, some output is always lost, e.g. in animals migrating away or nutrients being washed away in rivers.

B7 Further Biology (Learning from Ecosystems)

Products from Ecosystems

Natural ecosystems are important to humans as they provide…

- food, e.g. fish, game animals, pollination of crop plants by bees and moths
- clean air and oxygen from the actions of plants and microorganisms
- clean water.

Human Impact on Ecosystems

Human activity can upset the natural balance by changing the inputs and outputs of an ecosystem.

Examples of input change include…

- using fertilisers – minerals (e.g. phosphates and nitrates) in fertilisers can be washed into rivers and streams, leading to the water becoming stagnant and unable to support life
- burning fossil fuels – adds carbon dioxide to the atmosphere and increases climate change
- domestic and industrial waste – releases chemicals into the ecosystem, which may be harmful.

Examples of output change include…

- removal of non-recycled waste
- timber harvesting – removing trees for use in paper and furniture
- fishing – depleting stocks of fish for food
- agriculture – removing natural vegetation for crops (e.g. palm oil) or livestock (e.g. cattle).

This all means that human activity in systems **isn't** closed because input and output **aren't** balanced.

Removal of Vegetation

Removing vegetation may cause the following:

- Soil erosion – natural vegetation binds the soil together by the root systems and foliage protects the soil from direct rainfall. Without these, the soil can be washed away leading to **desertification**. The soil that is eroded can silt up rivers causing them to change course or to lose flow rate, affecting the aquatic life.
- Loss of biodiversity – the different plants in vegetation support many food chains and provide habitats for a wide variety of organisms. Replacing them with a crop or livestock reduces the diversity of plants and animals.
- Build-up of carbon dioxide – as less photosynthesis occurs, less carbon dioxide is removed from the atmosphere. It accumulates in the atmosphere, causing climate change (the **greenhouse effect**).
- Changes in weather – temperature and rainfall are both affected by vegetation such as rainforests. The trees lose water, which causes cloud formation and leads to rain (a freshwater supply) in other areas. Rainforests help to prevent temperature extremes as the density of vegetation keeps temperatures stable.

Over-fishing

Over-fishing may cause the following:

- Loss of biodiversity, leading to a reduction in food resources.
- Accumulation of organisms that would have been eaten by fish may have harmful effects on the resources available.

Desertification • Greenhouse effect

HT Eutrophication

Minerals may get washed away (**leached**) from fields into rivers and streams. In slow or non-flowing water (e.g. a lake), the build-up of minerals allows algae to grow at a fast rate:

1. At first, the fast growth of algae promotes life as more food is available.
2. As the algae die, the microorganisms of decay use up oxygen in the water in respiration.
3. The reduction in oxygen levels causes larger organisms to die. They, in turn decay, using up more oxygen.
4. The process leads to oxygen levels so low that life can't exist.

This is a slow process called **eutrophication**.

Bioaccumulation in Food Chains

Bioaccumulation occurs in the following way:

1. Small amounts of toxic waste may be taken up by plants and stored in their leaves, fruit or seeds.
2. Animals eat these plants and, as they eat a lot of plants, the amount of chemical stored in their bodies is higher than in a single plant.
3. These animals are eaten by other animals, so their bodies accumulate even higher levels of chemical.
4. The animals at the top of the food chain can become badly affected as the chemical reaches a harmful level in their bodies.

Examples of the effect of bioaccumulation at the top of food chains include…

- sparrowhawk egg-shells becoming brittle and breaking when the female sits on them, causing the number of sparrowhawks to reduce
- high mercury levels in some humans, which have been linked to psychological problems and even death.

Sustainable Development

Using natural resources can only be **sustainable** if the materials are replaced at the same rate they're used.

Using oil can't be sustainable as…

- crude oil takes millions of years to form from the decay of dead organisms
- the energy released from burning oil was 'fossil sunlight energy' as it originated from the Sun when the organisms were alive.

The removal of trees can be sustainable, if new trees are replanted as older ones are felled. Fish stocks can be kept at sustainable levels by the use of **quotas** (i.e. restricting the amount of fish allowed to be caught), so that the remaining fish can reproduce to replace those caught. Fish can be grown in artificial conditions and used to **restock** over-fished areas. In these ways, humans can at least try to 'close the loop'.

There will always be conflict between the needs of local human communities and the need to conserve the natural ecosystem. So, it's important that compromises are reached, which support the livelihoods of local people **and**, at the same time, maintain the balance of the ecosystem.

It's important to remember that…

- radiation from the Sun is the energy source for most biological systems on Earth
- energy can only be transformed or transferred; it can't be created or destroyed.

Quick Test

1. Why does the removal of trees and vegetation cause soil erosion?
2. Why is there no waste in a perfect closed loop system?
3. Why are decomposer organisms, such as fungi, so important to ecosystems?
4. How does the use of quotas in sea fishing help to sustain stocks?

Fermentation

A **fermenter** is a **controlled environment** that has ideal conditions for microorganisms to live in, feed and produce the proteins needed.

Fermenters can be used to grow **microorganisms,** and produce industrial quantities of products such as…

- **antibiotics** and other medicines
- **single-cell proteins**, for example, mycoprotein (the main ingredient of Quorn™, a meat substitute)
- **enzymes** that can be used in food production, for example, **chymosin**, a vegetarian substitute for rennet, which is used in cheese-making
- **enzymes** that can be used in washing powders to digest stains (mainly proteins)
- **enzymes** to make biofuels, such as ethanol (from the fermentation of sugar) to use in cars, or methane gas (from the fermentation of waste) to produce electricity.

Using Bacteria

Bacteria are ideal for using in genetic and industrial processes because…

- they have a very **simple** biochemistry, making them easier to work with
- they **reproduce very rapidly** and so produce the end product of the process quickly and in large amounts
- they have the ability to **make complex molecules** from simple ones
- they possess **DNA as plasmids** for ease of modification
- there is **no ethical opposition** to their culture, unlike the use of animals for example.

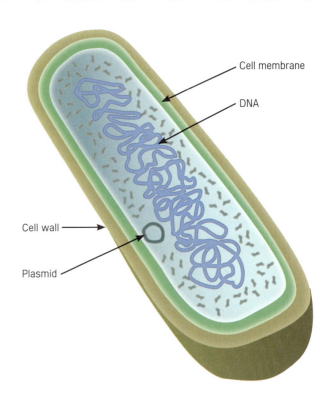

Cell membrane

DNA

Cell wall

Plasmid

B7 Further Biology (New Technologies)

Genetic Modification

DNA contains the code for the protein a particular organism needs. Proteins produced by one organism may not be produced by another.

By carrying out **genetic modification**, the gene that produces a desirable protein can be inserted into another organism so that it too produces the right protein.

This is how genetic modification is carried out:

1. The desired gene is selected and **isolated**.
2. The desired gene is inserted into a suitable **vector**, i.e. a **virus** or a **plasmid** (circular DNA molecule found in some bacteria).
3. The vector is allowed to reproduce.
4. Vectors carrying the desired gene are **inserted** into new cells, e.g. bacterial or plant cells.
5. From all the resulting individuals, those showing the modified characteristics are selected.

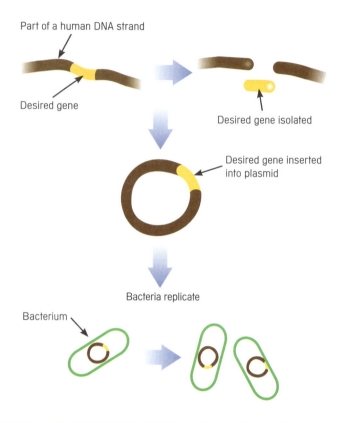

Part of a human DNA strand

Desired gene

Desired gene isolated

Desired gene inserted into plasmid

Bacteria replicate

Bacterium

Uses of Genetic Modification

Genetic modification has the potential to solve many problems for society. For example, it can be used to...

- produce healthier crops with greater yields
- produce disease-resistant crops, which reduces the need for pollution-causing pesticides
- enable some crops (e.g. bananas) to naturally carry vaccines so they don't need to be kept refrigerated
- allow organisations to monitor the release and spread of genetically modified crops by looking for antibiotic-resistant markers in crops (the markers will only be there if the crop has been modified)
- enable some drugs (e.g. insulin) to be made from human, rather than animal, DNA
- make some crops resistant to a herbicide, so that all other plants are killed by spraying and not the crop, leading to higher yields and easier harvesting.

HT Genetic Testing

The following method is used to test a gene:

1. DNA is isolated from the nucleus of a white blood cell. The DNA is often amplified so that there's enough material to experiment with. It's then broken up into different sized pieces.
2. A gene probe is created. This is a single-stranded DNA or RNA sequence that has bases that pair up with the complementary bases on the target gene. The probe will only attach if the desired gene is present in a sample and so acts as a marker.
3. Ultraviolet (UV) light is used to locate the marker if the probe has a marker that causes it to fluoresce when UV light is shone onto it.

Genetic modification • Vector

Nanotechnology

Nanotechnology…

- is the science of working with extremely small structures (only the size of some molecules)
- can be used in many different ways, including in medicine and the food industry.

Examples of the application of nanotechnology in the food industry include the following:

- Building **biosensors** in packaging to monitor food quality by detecting harmful microorganisms and perhaps changing colour as a warning. This ensures that the microorganisms don't enter the food chain and extends the **shelf-life** of the food, i.e. how long it stays safe and edible.
- Using **nanoparticles** in packaging, e.g. adding silver to act as an antimicrobial coating to stop decay organisms attacking the food and increasing its shelf-life.

Biosensors

Wrapping is clear

Wrapping has turned red due to biosensor detecting harmful microorganisms

Stem Cell Technology

Stem cells…

- are those cells that are completely unspecialised
- can potentially develop into any specialised cell
- can be found in developing embryos, umbilical cord and in adult tissues, e.g. bone marrow.

Stem cell technology has many potential applications, including the following:

- **Bone marrow transplants** – stem cells can be used to stimulate the regeneration of white blood cells in the treatment of **leukaemia** (blood cancer).
- Treating **spinal cord injuries** – stem cells can heal the damage by helping to regenerate neurons.
- Using **cell culture** – stem cells can be grown and transformed into new tissues or organs, e.g. skin and cornea for transplant in the treatment of burns and blindness.

Biomedical Engineering

Biomedical engineering involves using engineering techniques and ideas to solve medical problems. It has many branches but includes…

- **pacemakers** – electrical devices, usually implanted under the skin, to replace the heart's own pacemaker region, the sinoatrial node, to maintain an adequate and regular heartbeat
- replacement **heart valves** – devices that keep the blood flow within the heart efficient if a natural valve malfunctions.

Quick Test

1. What are containers of growing microorganisms that make products useful to industry, e.g. enzymes, called?
2. What is genetic modification?
3. What is nanotechnology?
4. What are unspecialised cells that have the potential to become any specialised cell called?

1. The graph on the right shows the maximum heart rate of four males during a single period of identical exercise and the time it took to fully return to resting rate afterwards.

   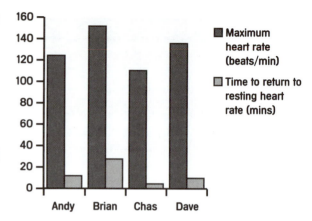

   (a) It was concluded that Chas was the fittest of the four men. Suggest a reason why this was not a good conclusion. **[1]**

   (b) Andy says that Brian should be worried. Using the data in the graph, suggest two reasons why Andy says this. **[2]**

   (c) Brian had his BMI (body mass index) checked and it was found to be 28. Use the BMI table below to suggest whether he should be concerned about his body mass. **[2]**

BMI	Condition
Under 19	Underweight
19–24	Normal weight
25–29	Overweight
30–40	Obese
Over 40	Severely obese

2. The students below are discussing closed loop systems in ecosystems.

   Jack
   Burying plastic waste in landfill is part of a closed loop system.

   Deborah
   The carbon cycle is part of a closed loop system.

   Will
   The nitrogen cycle is part of a closed loop system.

   Poppy
   Burning fossil fuels like coal is part of a closed loop system.

   Louis
   Natural ecosystems aren't closed loop systems.

   Which two students are giving correct statements? **[2]**

   _____ and _____

3 Nanotechnology could deliver improvements to our lives. However, some people say that it is 'not worth the risk'. Explain why we can't remove all risk and what policy-makers have to consider before going ahead. **[6]**

🖉 *The quality of written communication will be assessed in your answer to this question.*

....

....

....

....

....

....

....

....

....

HT **4** When cows die in India, they're sometimes eaten by vultures or wild dogs. Vultures will also eat dead dogs. To stop cows from catching certain diseases, a drug, called diclofenac, is given to them. Later on, some of these cows die of natural causes.

(a) Explain why, when tested, vultures contain a higher concentration of diclofenac than cows. **[2]**

....

....

(b) Some vultures die as a result of high drug levels. Why might this be important for humans? **[1]**

....

....

5 In the organs, capillary beds allow exchange of substances between the cells and the blood.

Describe how this exchange occurs, giving two examples of substances that pass between the cells and blood. **[4]**

....

....

....

....

....

Answers

Module B1: You and Your Genes

Quick Test Answers

Page 7

1. A long strand of DNA.
2. Different versions of the same gene.
3. Someone who could possibly pass on the disease to a child, but doesn't have it themselves.
4. The characteristics that an individual shows.

Page 11

1. Because the allele for Huntington's disease is dominant.
2. **Any two from:** Weight loss; Breathing difficulty; Chest infection; Difficulty digesting food
3. To see if the fetus has any faulty alleles/genes.
4. An unspecialised cell
5. An adult stem cell

Exam Practice Answers

1. **(a)** proteins **should be ringed.**
   (b) alleles
   (c) (i)

   Parent with Brown Eyes

	B	**b**
b	Bb	bb
B	BB	Bb

   (Left label: Parent with Brown Eyes)

   (ii) 75%

2. chromosomes; asexual; clones; environmental
   [2 marks if four correct; 1 mark if two correct]
3. True positive – Fetus **has** the disorder – Fetus **has** the disorder
   True negative – Fetus **doesn't** have the disorder – Fetus **doesn't** have the disorder
   False positive – Fetus **has** the disorder – Fetus **doesn't** have the disorder
   False negative – Fetus **doesn't** have the disorder – Fetus **has** the disorder
   [1 mark for matching each outcome with correct test result and reality]
4. **This is a model answer which would score full marks:**
   Huntington's disease is an incurable genetic disorder that causes suffering. However, people with the condition don't develop it until later life. It would be unethical to abort a fetus carrying the disorder as it could lead a normal life if allowed to develop as normal. Another issue is that the genetic test may be incorrect, giving a false positive, and a healthy fetus could then be aborted. **A good answer could also mention 'phenotype' and 'genotype'.**
5. Half the sperm carry an X chromosome and half the sperm carry a Y chromosome **[1]**. All the eggs (ova) carry an X chromosome **[1]**, so which type of sperm fertilises the egg decides whether the baby is female (XX) or male (XY) **[1]**.
6. **Any one from:** Genetic make-up; Types of alleles present (in the nucleus)

Module B2: Keeping Healthy

Quick Test Answers

Page 17

1. Virus
2. Warmth, moisture and nutrients (food)
3. White blood cell
4. Antigens
5. They are resistant to antibiotics.

Page 21

1. The left and right sides of the heart pump blood to different parts of the body.
2. Pressure as the heart is contracting.
3. Homeostasis

Exam Practice Answers

1. **(a)** A general increase over the period.
   (b) Any one from: Men in 2004; Women in 2005
   (c) Any two from: Poor diet; Smoking; Stress; Genetics; Drug abuse **[do not accept 'microbes / disease']**
   (d) Any one from: There is no data to correlate with alcohol consumption; There may have been more alcohol-related deaths not recorded in this study.

2. **(a)** B D A C **[1 mark for D before A; 1 mark for A before C]**
   (b) (i) White blood cell
   (ii) Antibody
   (iii) Antigen
   (iv) Microorganism
3. **(a)** A weakened or dead strain of the disease-causing microorganism **should be ticked.**
   (b) (i) There is a small chance of side effects occurring.
   (ii) The virus causing the disease mutates, producing a new strain that's unaffected by the current vaccine.
4. **(a) (i)** correlation **should be ringed.**
   (ii) possibly does not cause **should be ringed.**
   (b) (i) a harmless drug **should be ringed.**
   (ii) causes **should be ringed.**
5. **Any three points from:** Receptors **[1]** in the hypothalamus **[1]** cause less ADH production **[1]**, so the kidneys reabsorb less water **[1]** and larger amounts of urine are produced **[1]**.

Answers

Module B3: Life on Earth

Quick Test Answers

Page 28
1. Similar individuals capable of interbreeding to produce fertile offspring.
2. The leaves are reduced to spines.
3. Feeding relationships between organisms.
4. The Sun
5. An animal that consumes other organisms.
6. Dead organisms

Page 35
1. Photosynthesis
2. When individuals have characteristics that suit their environment / increase their chances of survival in an environment.
3. Charles Darwin
4. Meeting people's needs without damaging the Earth's environment for future generations.
5. Remove nitrogen from the air.
6. Denitrification

Exam Practice Answers
1. **This is a model answer which would score full marks:** The polar bear's white fur will help to camouflage it, so that it can catch prey more easily, and its teeth and claws will help it to eat the seals it catches. Its feet are rough to help it grip the ice and the claws will add to this grip and also help it to hold any seal it catches. The polar bear's fat layer and insulating fur keep it warm. The size of its nose and ears will help to cut down heat loss, as they have a small surface area exposed to the cold air.

2. **(a)** As sulfur dioxide levels decrease, the number of lichen species increases.
   (b) Any one from: No indication is given of how much lichen is present (only number of species); Sulfur dioxide levels may have been taken on only one occasion / may not be representative.
   (c) Indicator species
   (d) Industry / Pollution is found in the town centre.

3.

Cabbage	A		Shark	H
Human	H		Ant	H
Elm tree	A		Orchid	A

[3 marks if six correct; 2 marks if four correct; 1 mark if two correct]

4. **(a) Any three from:** Increased competition; New predators; Changes to the environment; New diseases; Human activities, e.g. industry, deforestation
   (b) Mutations (in genes)
5. **(a)** Photosynthesis
   (b) $23\,400 - (3600 + 3050 + 14\,790) = 1960\text{kJ}$
   (c) $\frac{120}{3050} \times 100 = 3.9\%$
   [1 mark for correct working but wrong answer]
6. **(a)** It converts atmospheric nitrogen to nitrates (nitrogen compounds).
   (b) It converts soil nitrates to atmospheric nitrogen.

Module B4: The Processes of Life

Quick Test Answers

Page 41
1. (They contain the enzymes for) aerobic respiration.
2. Cell wall, chloroplasts and permanent vacuole
3. Protein molecules that speed up reactions in cells / act as catalysts in living things.
4. The release of energy (from food chemicals) in all living cells.
5. Anaerobic respiration doesn't use oxygen, whereas aerobic does use oxygen.
6. Denatured

Page 45
1. Chlorophyll
2. Oxygen
3. Nitrates
4. **Any one from:** A random section across an area; A representative area to sample.
5. The movement of substances from a region of high concentration to an area of low concentration.
6. Water

Exam Practice Answers
1. **(a) (i)** C **(ii)** D
   (b) They contain the enzymes for (aerobic) respiration.
2. **(a)** The greater the light intensity, the faster the rate of photosynthesis.
   (b) Oxygen
   (c) Any one from: Carbon dioxide; Temperature
3. Ethanol is produced as a waste product **should be ticked**.
4. **(a) Any one from:** To ensure that they weren't different; To ensure they were the same type/consistency; To ensure they didn't 'react' differently.
   (b) Water had entered the potato (cells).
   (c) Water had moved out of the potato (cells).
5. **(a)** Oxygen; Carbon dioxide; Dissolved food
   (b) partially; dilute; concentrated; osmosis **[2 marks if four correct; 1 mark if two correct]**
6. **(a)** Sebastian; Nicholas
   (b) It's where an enzyme is permanently destroyed and stops working.

87

Answers

Module B5: Growth and Development

Quick Test Answers
Page 51
1. A group of similar cells (to perform a function).
2. Mitosis
3. Testes and ovaries
4. Zygote
5. bases
6. Messenger RNA / mRNA

Page 55
1. Meristems
2. Xylem (vessels)
3. Phloem
4. Hormone / Auxin
5. Phototropism

Exam Practice Answers
1. (a) [B] [D] [C] [A]
   [1 mark for D before C; 1 mark for C before A]
   (b) Testes; Ovaries
   (c) Zygote

2. **This is a model answer which would score full marks:** The Sun shining on the plant from only one side would mean that it would grow towards the light. This is because the growth rate on the dark side is much faster than on the light side. This pattern of growth is called phototropism and is caused by hormones. It helps the plant to obtain more sunlight energy for photosynthesis. This allows the plant to produce more glucose, giving it more energy for growth and reproduction, and helping it to survive.
   A good answer could also include the following point: Auxin being destroyed by light, promoting growth on the dark side.
3. (a) They're unspecialised and can turn into any kind of cell.
   (b) The cells will have become specialised.
   (c) Embryonic stem cells can develop into any specialised cell, whereas adult stem cells can only develop into some specialised cells.
4. (a) **Any two from:** B quadruples every 30 minutes, whereas D does not; The growth of B is constant, whereas D changes; The growth of B is faster than D; B has 12 division cycles, whereas D has 10 cycles.
   (b) (In all four cases the number quadrupled in this time). **Any one from:** B / D also quadrupled between 0 and 30 minutes; D also quadrupled between 90 and 120 minutes and/or between 150 and 180 minutes; B quadrupled every time.
5. (a) Chloe; Emily
   (b) mRNA is a smaller copy that is small enough to leave.

Module B6: Brain and Mind

Quick Test Answers
Page 61
1. A change in an organism's environment.
2. Motor neuron
3. Synapse
4. Axon
5. A fast, automatic, involuntary response to a stimulus.
6. Conditioned reflex action

Page 65
1. Neuron pathways
2. Cerebral cortex
3. MRI (Magnetic Resonance Imaging)
4. The ability to store and retrieve information.
5. Short-term memory
6. They affect the passage of an impulse across a synapse.

Exam Practice Answers
1. (a) (i) central nervous system **should be ringed**.
       (ii) peripheral nervous system **should be ringed**.
   (b) (i) Sensory neuron
       (ii) Motor neuron
   (c) It causes the gland to release a hormone into the blood.
   (d) It insulates the neuron; It increases the speed at which the impulse travels.
   (e) Synapses are the gaps between adjacent neurons.
   (f) They change the speed at which nerve impulses travel to the brain.

2. **This is a model answer which would score full marks:** When Raul picks up the plate, receptors in his skin will be stimulated to set up an impulse in a sensory neuron. This impulse will move across a synapse to a relay neuron in his spinal cord and then across a second synapse to set up an impulse in a motor neuron. This impulse will pass to muscles in his arm, causing contraction, resulting in him moving his fingers to release the hot plate.
   A good answer could also include the following point: Neurotransmitters also diffuse across the synapse.
3. (a) 1.32 in small dose
   (b) The drug slows down the reaction time.
   (c) **Any one from:** So that it's a good estimate of the true reaction time; Repeatability reduces the chances of a false result. **[Do not accept 'to make it a fair test'.]**
4. have a scientific mechanism; be published; **and** be repeatable **should be ticked. [2 marks for all three; 1 mark for two]**
5. (a) [D] [B] [E] [C] [A] **[1 mark for B before E; 1 mark for E before C; 1 mark for C before A]**
   (b) Ecstasy (MDMA)

Answers

Module B7: Further Biology

Quick Test Answers

Page 73

1. Tendons
2. Antagonistic pair
3. BMI = $\dfrac{\text{Body mass (kg)}}{[\text{Height (m)}]^2}$
4. **Any three from:** Swelling; Redness; Warmth; Pain at the joint
5. They carry oxygen around the body.
6. Aorta

Page 76

1. Heat is released into the blood as a result of increased respiration.
2. Insulin
3. Type 1 occurs when the pancreas stops producing enough insulin, whereas type 2 occurs when the body stops responding to its own insulin or doesn't make enough insulin.
4. Complex carbohydrates release sugar slowly, whereas simple carbohydrates release sugar rapidly.

Page 80

1. The roots bind the soil together and without them the soil is washed away. The leaves also protect the soil from direct rainfall.
2. Any waste output is used as input in another part of the system.
3. They break down waste materials and dead organisms so the products can be recycled.
4. It allows fish to remain and reproduce to increase populations.

Page 83

1. Fermenters
2. Changing the genetic make-up / genotype of an organism
3. The science of working with extremely small structures
4. Stem cells

Exam Practice Answers

1. **(a) Any one from:** There is no data about the size / weight / age of the men; The exercise test was not repeated so these may not be the true values.
   (b) Brian's heart rate is very high during exercise and he takes a long time to recover **[1]**, and both are indicators of poor fitness levels **[1]**.
   (c) Brian is in the overweight range **[1]**, but he is near the top of the range so if he gains much more weight he will be obese **[1]**.
2. Deborah; Will
3. **This is a model answer which would score full marks:** Nothing is without risk – even not doing something carries a risk. Sometimes we don't even know what the risks are until they happen. The consequences of some risks can be greater than others, so policy-makers have to balance the potential risk with the potential benefit. If the benefits are greater and will help many people, then it can go ahead.
4. **(a)** Cows containing diclofenac are eaten by vultures **[1]** and, as they eat more cows, the drug accumulates in their bodies **[1]**.
   (b) Because the drug may accumulate in humans and cause harm if they eat cows / beef.
5. Substances like glucose and oxygen **[1]** diffuse **[1]** out of the blood into the tissue fluid **[1]** surrounding the cells and then into the cells for use. Substances like urea and carbon dioxide **[1]** diffuse out of the cells into the tissue fluid and then into the blood for removal.
   [1 mark for each named substance up to a maximum of 2]

Glossary of Key Words

Adult stem cell – a cell able to differentiate, originating from an adult cell.

Aerobic respiration – respiration using oxygen; releases energy and produces carbon dioxide and water.

Allele – an alternative form of a particular gene.

Anaerobic respiration – the process of releasing energy from glucose in living cells in the absence of oxygen to produce a small amount of energy very quickly.

Antagonistic pair – a pair of muscles that work together to create movement: when one contracts, the other relaxes.

Antibiotic – a type of antimicrobial that kills bacteria and fungi, but not viruses.

Antibody – produced by white blood cells to inactivate disease-causing microorganisms.

Antigen – a marker on the surface of a disease-causing microorganism.

Antimicrobial – a chemical that kills bacteria, fungi and viruses.

Artery – a muscular blood vessel that carries blood away from the heart.

Asexual reproduction – new offspring are reproduced that are identical to the parent.

Atrium – one of the upper chambers of the heart, which receives blood coming back to the heart.

Autotroph – an organism that makes its own food.

Axon – the thread-like extension of a nerve cell.

Bacteria – single-celled microorganisms with no nucleus.

Biodegradable – a material that decomposes naturally.

Biodiversity – the range of species in an environment.

Biomedical engineering – using artificial devices to replace natural parts of an organism.

Body mass index (BMI) – a measure of fitness.

Bone – rigid connective tissue that makes up the human skeleton.

Capillary – a blood vessel that connects arteries to veins; where the exchange of materials takes place.

Carnivore – an organism that eats other animals; a secondary or tertiary consumer.

Central nervous system – the brain and spinal cord; allows an organism to react to its surroundings and coordinates its responses.

Cerebral cortex – the part of the human brain most concerned with intelligence, memory, language and consciousness.

Chlorophyll – the green pigment found in most plants; responsible for photosynthesis.

Chromosome – a long molecule found in the nucleus of all cells containing DNA.

Clinical trial – the process of testing a medical treatment or medicine on human volunteers for safety and effectiveness.

Clone – an organism genetically identical to the parent.

Closed loop system – an ecosystem where waste from one part is used by another.

Combustion – burning in oxygen / air.

Common ancestor – the most recent individual from which all organisms in a group are directly descended.

Conditioned reflex – a reflex action brought about by a learned stimulus.

Cystic fibrosis – a recessive hereditary disorder that mainly affects the lungs and digestive system.

Decomposer – an organism that breaks down dead materials and waste products.

Deoxygenated – a substance low in oxygen.

Desertification – turning land to desert conditions.

Diabetes – a medical condition where blood sugar levels are too high.

Diagnosis – the decision reached regarding the identification of a condition.

Diffusion – the net movement of particles from an area of high concentration to an area of low concentration.

Dislocation – the displacement of a part, especially the displacement of a bone at the joint.

DNA (deoxyribonucleic acid) – molecules that code for genetic information and make up chromosomes.

Double circulation system – blood returns to the heart twice on each circuit of the body.

Ecosystem – a term that refers to a physical environment, including the conditions there and the organisms that live there.

Effector – the part of the body, e.g. a muscle or a gland, which produces a response to a stimulus.

Embryo – a ball of cells that will develop into a human / animal baby.

Embryonic stem cell – a cell able to differentiate, originating from an embryo cell.

Energy – the ability to do work; measured in joules (J).

Environmental variation – variation that occurs as a result of a certain factor in the surroundings.

Enzyme – a protein that speeds up the rate of reaction in living organisms (a catalyst in living things).

Epidemiological study – a study of the factors affecting the health and illness of populations.

Evolution – the gradual process of adaptation of a species over generations.

Excretion – the removal of waste products of cell reactions.

Extinction – the process by which groups of organisms die out.

Fermenter – a controlled environment that maintains ideal conditions for microorganisms to carry out fermentation.

Fertilisation – the fusion of the male gamete with the female gamete.

Fetus – an unborn human / animal baby.

Food chain – a simple chain showing the feeding relationship between organisms in an ecosystem.

Food web – interlinked food chains in an ecosystem.

Fossil – animal / plant remains preserved in rock.

Fungi – a group of organisms including mushrooms, toadstools and yeasts.

Gamete – a specialised sex cell formed by meiosis.

Gene – a small section of DNA of a chromosome that determines a particular characteristic.

Genetic modification – the change in the genetic make-up of an organism.

Greenhouse effect – climate change / global warming due to pollution.

Herbivore – an organism that only eats plants, grass, etc; a primary consumer.

Heterotroph – an organism that is unable to make its own food; consumes other organisms.

Homeostasis – the maintenance of a constant internal environment.

Hormone – a regulatory substance that stimulates cells or tissues into action.

Huntington's disease – a hereditary, degenerative disorder of the central nervous system.

Immune system – the body's defence system against infections and diseases (consists of white blood cells and antibodies).

Indicator organism – an organism that is only found in certain conditions.

Glossary of Key Words

Insulin – a hormone that causes sugar to be taken from blood.

Kingdom – a classification of a group of organisms with a small number of features in common.

Ligament – the tissue that connects a bone to a joint.

Meiosis – the cell division that forms daughter cells with half the number of chromosomes as the parent cell.

Memory – the ability to store and retrieve information.

Meristem – an area where unspecialised cells divide, producing plant growth.

Mitosis – the cell division that forms two daughter cells, each with the same number of chromosomes as the parent cell.

Muscle – tissue that can contract and relax to produce movement.

Mutation – a spontaneous change in the genetic code of a cell.

Nanotechnology – the science of working with structures that are extremely small.

Natural immunity – to remain resistant to or be unaffected by a specific disease.

Natural selection – a natural process resulting in the evolution of organisms best adapted to the environment.

Neuron – a specialised cell that transmits electrical messages or nerve impulses when stimulated.

Nucleus – the control centre of a cell, containing DNA.

Organ – a collection of tissues to carry out a function.

Organelles – the different parts of a cell's structure.

Osmosis – the movement of water from a dilute to a more concentrated solution across a partially permeable membrane.

Oxygenated – a substance rich in oxygen.

Oxyhaemoglobin – haemoglobin with oxygen bound on.

Photosynthesis – the chemical process that takes place in green plants where water combines with carbon dioxide to produce glucose using light.

Phototropism – a plant's response to light.

Pollution – harmful additions to the environment.

Polymer – a large molecule made up from many similar units (monomers).

Protein – large organic compounds made of amino acids.

Quadrat – a defined area used to sample a location.

Receptor – the part of the nervous system that detects a stimulus.

Reflex action – a fast, automatic response.

Selective breeding – the production of new varieties of animals and plants by artificial selection.

Side effect – a condition caused by taking medication, e.g. headache, nausea.

Species – similar organisms capable of interbreeding to produce fertile offspring.

Sprain – a stretch or tear in a ligament.

Stem cell – a cell of a human embryo or adult bone marrow that has the ability to differentiate.

Stimulus – a change in an organism's environment.

Sustainable – capable of being continued with minimal long-term effect on the environment.

Symptom – a visible or noticeable effect of a disease, illness or injury.

Synapse – a small gap between adjacent neurons.

Tendon – tissue that connects a muscle to a bone.

Theory of evolution – the most likely scientific explanation, based on evidence, as to why organisms are the way they are.

Tissue – a collection of similar cells to carry out a function.

Transect – a fixed path across an area of study.

Valve – a device that ensures the flow of a liquid (e.g. blood) in the right direction.

Variation – differences between individuals of the same species.

Vector – an organism (often a microorganism) used to transfer a gene, or genes, from one organism to another.

Vein – a blood vessel that carries blood towards the heart.

Ventricle – one of the lower chambers of the heart, which pumps blood out of the heart.

Vertebrate – an organism with an internal skeleton.

Virus – a tiny microorganism with a very simple structure that is reliant on using a cell's machinery to reproduce.

White blood cell – a type of cell in blood that fights infection.

Zygote – a cell formed by the fusion of the nuclei of a male sex cell and a female sex cell (gametes).

Glossary of Key Words

HT **Active site** – the place where the molecule fits into the enzyme.

Active transport – the movement of a substance against a concentration gradient.

Anti-diuretic hormone (ADH) – a hormone that controls the concentration of urine.

Auxin – a plant hormone that affects the growth and development of a plant.

Bioaccumulation – the build-up of toxic materials inside living cells.

Denatured enzyme – an enzyme that has had its shape destroyed and can no longer catalyse reactions.

Denitrification – taking nitrogen from materials, e.g. nitrates.

Detritivore – an animal that feeds on dead materials.

Eutrophication – the process that leads to stagnation of fresh water.

Genotype – the genetic make-up of an organism.

Heterozygous – when a pair of alleles for a characteristic are different.

Homozygous – when a pair of alleles for a characteristic are the same.

Hypothalamus – the part of the brain responsible for maintaining homeostasis.

***In vitro* fertilisation (IVF)** – a technique in which egg cells are fertilised outside the female body.

Messenger RNA (mRNA) – the molecule that carries the genetic code out of the nucleus.

Nitrogen fixing – the removal of nitrogen from the air.

Phenotype – the characteristics shown by an individual.

Pituitary gland – the small gland at the base of the brain that produces hormones.

Pre-implantation Genetic Diagnosis (PGD) – involves removing a cell from an embryo at an early stage of development and testing it for genetic disorders.

Sex-determining region Y – a sex-determining gene on the Y chromosome in humans and other primates.

Therapeutic cloning – cloning a cell to make a healthy tissue to replace a damaged one.

Vasoconstriction – the narrowing of the blood vessels to decrease heat loss from the surface of the skin.

Vasodilation – the widening of the blood vessels to increase heat loss from the surface of the skin.

Notes

Index